The Risk in Crime

The Risk in Crime

Leslie W. Kennedy and
Erin Gibbs Van Brunschot

ROWMAN & LITTLEFIELD PUBLISHERS, INC.
Lanham • Boulder • New York • Toronto • Plymouth, UK

Published by Rowman & Littlefield Publishers, Inc.
A wholly owned subsidiary of The Rowman & Littlefield Publishing Group, Inc.
4501 Forbes Boulevard, Suite 200, Lanham, Maryland 20706
http://www.rowmanlittlefield.com

Estover Road, Plymouth PL6 7PY, United Kingdom

British Library Cataloguing in Publication Information Available

Library of Congress Cataloging-in-Publication Data

Kennedy, Leslie W.
 The risk in crime / Leslie W. Kennedy and Erin Gibbs Van Brunschot.
   p. cm.
 Includes bibliographical references and index.
  ISBN 978-1-4422-0053-1 (cloth : alk. paper) — ISBN 978-1-4422-0054-8 (pbk. : alk. paper)— ISBN 978-1-4422-0055-5 (electronic)
 1. Crime. 2. Crime prevention. 3. Risk—Sociological aspects. 4. Risk assessment. 5. Risk management. 6. Criminal justice, Administration of. I. Van Brunschot, Erin Gibbs. II. Title.
 HV6025.K293 2009
 364.01—dc22
                                          2009019889

Contents

Preface

This is the book that we meant to write about ten years ago when we became interested in the role that risk plays in crime. We had put together some ideas, talked a lot about risky lifestyles, public anxieties and fear, and multiple victimization, thinking that these ideas were well researched but poorly accounted for in criminological thinking. Also, there seemed a disconnect between what we knew about victims and offenders and how we understood what police did in trying to control crime and mitigate its effects on society. There was not enough attention paid to the risk assessments that police and others involved in social control make, even if these were not explicitly labeled as risk assessments, either in police training or practice.

We felt there was a need to address these ideas, sensing that in the confusing landscape of conflicting criminological theories, there was a real possibility that we could tie some of these ideas together using the insights drawn from the risk literature. Work on risk has developed into a large industry applied in a variety of ways and locations; most recently, it has made its way into strategic planning and how corporations need to manage their assets and protect their interests. It also has roots in human health, disaster planning, and emergency response literatures. So, as we began to read this work, we found ourselves distracted by and into these topics, trying to locate crime research in the overall interdisciplinary study of risk. This study of risk led us to the work on "risk society" that has been developed by global thinkers such as Ulrich Beck (1992), who alerts us to major changes in the ways that we view society—from fatalistic to interventionist perspectives—which impact on the ways in which societies approach risk. Risk society theorizing is more about control and less about individual choice. Risk society literature led us to circle back to individuals and their risk perceptions, guided most notably by the work of Amos Tversky, Daniel Kahneman, and Paul Slovic, who have studied the intricacies of how individuals come to understand risk processes. These researchers push back on the idea that risk is exclusively as experts see it but can, instead, be heavily influenced by the calculations that individuals themselves make about their lives and the strategies they develop in responding to their perceptions. Further, we became acutely aware that, as a background to the discussion of risk, there was a much larger debate about what to do about risk, which led us into a complex review of risk governance and, most specifically, the decisions that are made about the allocation of resources to respond to the hazards and opportunities that we face.

Our distraction led us to write a different book than the one we originally intended, one that tried to come to terms with the different pressures on society to manage hazards of all sorts through integrated risk management strategies and then to establish a form of "risk balance" that provides the stability we need to control the worst effects of these hazards. *Risk Balance and Security* (2008) was the result of this diversion, and while we paid attention to crime as one of the dangers we needed to address in risk management, the analysis was part of a larger interdisciplinary approach to security that painted a broad picture of how this should take place.

When the book was published, we were left with the original challenge that we had set for ourselves, which was to address how risk can be used as a key element in the understanding of crime origins, evolution, and prevention. So, we have returned to this topic, and in this book we deal with this issue in much greater detail than we were able to in *Risk Balance and Security*. This task was, surprisingly, a bit less challenging for us than the previous one, probably as we are more versed in crime theories than those about health and disease or disasters. But, also, the previous book posed the daunting task of making sense of security and the connection that this has to risk. Here, we have set as the job for ourselves the much more straightforward investigation of how risk has been dealt with in crime theories and the usefulness of this concept in connecting these ideas more closely together through the use of the criminal event perspective; the ways in which risk is embedded in the evolution of crime; and how we might use the concept of risk to prevent crime and victimization. The implicit notion of risk assessment practiced by police is explored and made explicit in our treatment of this topic in our last chapter.

We believe that the increased interest in risk demands that we have a clearer idea of how it works within crime theories and how it can be successfully employed in improving police practice, providing the tools to act proactively on good intelligence and carefully thought out strategies.

The authors would like to thank Alan McClare and his staff at Rowman & Littlefield for providing encouragement and support throughout this project.

Alan is the ideal editor: patient, intelligent, and encouraging. It was a pleasure doing business with him.

Les would like to thank, again, his coauthor and friend, Erin, for her continued support and patience as we career through the difficult job of writing. He knows she continues to enjoy the working trips to the New York area that, when work finishes, lead to great shopping and a few idle hours by the lake in Central Park. He would also like to thank the staff, students, and faculty at Rutgers School of Criminal Justice (SCJ) for their support, in particular Bil Leipold, who in his return to our school has brought a sense of order and decency that make going to work fun. Also, Norm Samuels gets thanks for his moral and intellectual guidance and Steve Diner for his support for the Center for Public Security and other initiatives at SCJ. They are both close and loyal friends. He thanks his colleagues who have added to his thinking about the ideas presented here including Vince Sacco, Ed McGarrell, Joel Caplan, Jean McGloin, Cynthia Lum, and Johnna Christian. He is also indebted to his many students who have tolerated his fixation on risk including Mark Anarumo, Chris Andreychak, Jie Xu, Renee Graphia, Jack Jarmon, and Heather Tubman Carbone. He thanks, as well, his many Turkish friends (most notably Suleyman Hancerli who made his recent trip to Turkey both educational and a marvelous tourist experience) and students (who he also categorizes as friends), Nyazi, Oghuzan, Sevki, Ahmet, Rhami, and Hakan. Of course, Ilona, Alexis, and Andrea get special thanks: he learns something new from each of them every day. Finally, to his late Mom and Dad, he acknowledges a deep debt for providing such great models to live by.

Erin would like to thank Les for his passion for their work, his insight, his patience, and his friendship, not to mention his superlative tour guide skills. Thanks to Kevin McQuillan for providing a daily dose of humor and support, and to the dean's office staff for making work a fun place to be. The "social club," including Gillian, Leslie, Gus, Dick, Kiara, Heather, and Ed, always supply a laugh and sense of perspective. Giorgia, Paige, Jesse, and Jim provide the "reality factor" with much love and encouragement, along with perceptive questions, as well as time to let Erin do what she thinks she needs to—thank you.

Finally, the authors are most grateful for the reviewers, in particular Chris Sullivan, who provided detailed comments that both clarified and refined our thinking about many parts of this book.

1

Introducing Risk

CALCULATING CRIME RISK

On the website Expert Business Source, under the title "Reducing the Risk of Crime in Your Store,"[1] there is a review of a number of steps that retail storeowners can take to deal with crime. They are encouraged to train staff, discuss problems with law enforcement, and reduce opportunities. Storeowners are discouraged from offering resistance during robberies and should refrain from using alarms until after the perpetrators have left the premises. Lighting should be adequate for surveillance, and there should be strong storage for valuables. Finally, proprietors are encouraged not to keep guns in the store. The implication of this advice is that, if the storeowners follow it, their risk of victimization will go down. While this seems like reasonable advice, not all of these recommendations relate specifically to the probability of crime occurring. Rather, they relate to other parts of the crime equation: what might happen prior to crime—the likelihood of deterring a crime, for example—or what might happen after a crime occurs (as a consequence of it), such as the degree of harm (low to high), the value of goods involved, the likelihood of success, and so forth. We could say that, from the offender's point of view, these steps make success less likely, but from the victim's point of view the offender may get fewer goods and do less harm.

In an article from a United Kingdom news source, Channel 4, a report indicated that "high-risk offenders" were guilty of committing one-third more violent crimes in July 2007, than in the previous year. The report states,

> There were 83 freed criminals charged with a further serious offence while under the supervision of the probation service and other agencies, compared with

1

61 in 2005/06. Twelve of those crimes were carried out by offenders among 1,249 assessed as the "critical few" with the highest risk of harming the public, and supposedly under the most rigorous supervision.[2]

In this case, risk is used to describe offenders who have previously acted violently, making them more likely to act in similar ways again (which, according to this report, they do). Risk, in these terms, describes characteristics of offenders that predict repetition of behavior, while in the store example above, risk relates to characteristics of environments that make them susceptible to crime and victims susceptible to harm. What is the connection between high-risk offenders and increased risk in particular premises? Let's look at another example.

While the high-risk offenders that we referred to above are judged because of their previous crimes, risk is also deduced from noncriminal behavior or from particular characteristics. In a study in the United Kingdom on children, everything from deprivation, location in high-crime areas, and problem behaviors were identified as risk markers—used to predict the risk of possible criminal behavior (a suggestion that has been made throughout the delinquency literature for decades; Armstrong et al. 2005).[3] Risk is used here to describe attributes of juvenile behavior or characteristics that make certain kids more likely to be in trouble or to commit crime. "Risk markers" serve as red flags to authorities to watch out for kids involved in specific behaviors or with particular characteristics, suggesting that those who participate in identified risk behavior, or live "risky lifestyles," are more likely to get into trouble.

As you can do on websites to judge your health risks, from being overweight or from living in polluted neighborhoods, a similar assessment can be made about your personal crime risk, that is, the likelihood of becoming a victim of crime. In a website called Rate Your Risk, Ken Pence provides a test for individuals to evaluate their chances of being victims of rape, robbery, stabbings, shootings, and beatings.[4] With the results of this test, a follow-up quiz is then taken to show how to avoid these threats to life and limb. Risk in this context revolves around the individual and focuses on people and things that he or she encounters in daily life that might precipitate a violent crime. In this case, risk is not so much focused on previous behavior by the individual (as is the case with high-risk offenders) as it focuses on previous victimization and living circumstances. In this context, risk has to do with exposure to harm rather than propensity to act.

Related to this, Robert Davis and Barbara Smith (1994) point out, "Data indicate that persons who become victims of crime run a higher than normal risk of becoming victims again. Because of their increased vulnerability to crime and their motivation to prevent future crimes, victims make an ideal population for training in crime prevention techniques."[5] The authors present findings from research experiments that exposed victims to a crime-prevention training program by asking them to consider how the crime that was perpetrated against them might have been prevented. Davis and Smith report that the program increased the participants' knowledge of crime-prevention principles and strengthened their understanding of precautionary behaviors. In addition, it reinforced participants' belief that future crime victimization could be avoided. Interestingly enough, the authors found that the program did not reduce the chances that the individuals involved in the study would be revictimized, nor did it reduce their fear.

The more complicated attempts at making sense of risk have developed "risk matrices" that combine factors that might contribute to crime occurrence.[6] Matrices developed by the United Kingdom's Home Office involve situational and social crime risk factors that can be used by schools and hospitals to identify the likelihood of crime occurring and the harm that would be done if it were to occur.[7] In addition, they include information about who is likely to commit the crime and when it may occur. The users are encouraged to go through a number of steps, including drawing up a list of previous incidents that have occurred in the school or hospital. Then, "by weighing up the impact and likelihood of the incident, the resultant risk matrix will help you to prioritize your future actions on your site." The risk matrices assume that future actions are based on previous events, an assumption that seems perfectly plausible and conforms to our everyday expectations. But can this be translated into measurable risk, and, if so, what action can be taken to stop the recurrence of these events?

In a different context, we can see that the elements that are attributed to creating risk of delinquency, for example, are also viewed negatively in more general terms—creating social instability and disorganization in neighborhoods, thereby increasing the likelihood of crime. An article by Adele Harrell and Caterina Gouvis (1994) focuses on the relationship between crime and urban decay. Urban decay involves measures of social disorganization, economic deprivation, and neighborhood structure and composition. In looking at the indicators of neighborhood decline, the authors set out models for predicting crime, suggesting that the disorder measures operate as risk factors potentially leading to criminal outcomes. This form of analysis has been popular since the mid-eighteenth century when Charles Booth (1879) studied the effects that concentrated poverty had on crime in London. In modern applications, the use of these urban decay correlates as defining factors in creating risky environments raises the possibility, as it did 130 years ago, that, if we are able to address disorder and the social confusion it creates, we would then have a better chance of reducing crime.

The challenge of dealing with crime risk can also be seen in the need to balance the cost of response against the likelihood of victimization. In other words, there are times when positions regarding "acceptable" risk must be taken, realizing that a certain amount of loss may occur in the normal course of business. We recognize, deal with, and define acceptable risks during the course of our everyday lives. But acceptable risks must be defined at all levels—not just by individuals. Institutions, governments, and states define levels of acceptable risk and weigh whether applying resources to lower risks is cost effective, including both social and economic costs. Certainly, when there are scarce police resources and limited funds for crime prevention, there may be an implicit decision taken that there can be a certain amount of acceptable risk that will have to be tolerated in certain areas.

CALCULATING LAW ENFORCEMENT RISK

Risk calculations are not only associated with individual or business circumstances. Risk can also play an important role in influencing the actions of law enforcement agencies. In its most basic form, policing is about response. Police agencies are structured to be vigilant for problems, to be quick to react to disorder and crime, and to provide assistance to people in distress (not always in the context of a criminal event). This is not to say that police do not seek to understand what causes crime or how to prevent it, but despite innovations that have sought to change policing to be more proactive, such as community policing, it has stayed predominantly in a reactive mode. Notwithstanding this position, police leaders have sought to move their organizations forward to more strategic planning and greater accountability of managers and officers for the crime that does occur. This search for accountability has had the effect of making police more likely to search for ways in which they can do their jobs more effectively.

At the end of the last century, two major changes took place in policing that brought about major modifications to the ways in which crime is managed and controlled. These changes can be framed in terms of risk assessment—a consideration of the probabilities of particular outcomes, both positive and negative—and should be considered in terms of their long-term impact on threats of crime and the resources available to respond to it through both prevention and enforcement.

The first change emerged from a technological innovation: the introduction in the late 1970s of the 911 telephone number that provided the public with immediate access to the police in an emergency (although it took until the late 1990s for this to be designated in the United States as a nationwide emergency system). At the time of the widespread introduction of this service, police agencies were immersed in ongoing discussions about response times and the need to provide uniform coverage throughout urban areas. The impact was that 911 calls broadened the focus of police from patrol and random surveillance to one that was based on the demands by the public for assistance. Initially, all calls for assistance were treated equally despite good evidence that policing, to be effective, needs to be targeted depending on the seriousness of the incident being reported. Yet the politics of the day demanded that the police give equal treatment to anyone in need, and they soon found themselves swamped with work, not all of which required their immediate attention. For example, calls for burglaries, after the intruder had long left the premises, ended up at the top of the list alongside calls for response to violent crimes where the assailant might still be in close proximity to the victim.

After finding that requests for more resources to respond to this huge and ever-growing demand would not be met by local authorities already straining to provide more costly services with limited means to meet the costs, police soon began to develop priority lists of calls. They quietly began a practice of using dispatchers to gauge call importance, employing a calculation of the amount of danger the situation posed to the victim; the consequences of not arriving in a timely way; and the caller's ability to deal with the problem on her or his own. This calculation of risk became a central part of the response strategies of police agencies imbedding decisions about the relative seriousness of incidents into police strategies. As this plan was initiated, there was an increasing engagement of the police with the public in a form of self-help, geared at prevention and encouraging citizen involvement in crime issues (see Kennedy and Veitch 1997). The overreliance on call centers dropped, as well, when municipalities began to implement customer service lines (such as 311) that quickly redirected the more serious police "emergencies" away from 911 dispatchers. Calling 311 would allow citizens to do everything from complaining about the police to requesting help in finding social services.

Also, in some jurisdictions, citizens who were crime victims might find that the police did not dispatch officers to deal with their complaints but the caller was, instead, encouraged to come down to a local police station to file the necessary paperwork for police follow-up. In all of these cases, the police determined that certain actions contained greater, and others less, risk to the victims and to the community. This radical departure in police practice did not go without comment in some communities that felt the police were ignoring their problems. Yet the reality of limited funding, the growth of community policing, and the apparent success of targeted policing that emerged from funneling resources to more serious events mollified most critics.

Interestingly enough, this shift in focus to consequences, although advocated by some researchers who saw randomized response as inefficient, seemed to escape the attention of many criminologists. Throughout the time frame of these changes, criminologists continued to focus on crime as a product of a constant supply of motivated offenders or broad-ranging available targets demanding police response as determined by the seriousness defined by crime situations. Little account was taken of the fact that crime now garnered police response based on seriousness defined by risk.

The changes brought about by the use of 911 were not the only factors leading to a shift in the impact that police had on crime. With the evolving view that police could be deployed more strategically, there was also, as we suggested above, the realization that accountability was needed to monitor the effectiveness of these shifts. This change involved not only redefining response to crime but also rethinking prevention. Police, through community policing strategies, began to realize that certain areas that produced a larger degree of crime needed special attention. This strategy, as we discuss later, did not target only serious crimes but also included a much broader surveillance strategy to deal with the correlates of crime: disorder and minor rule breaking.

To make sense of where to place resources in attacking disorder-based crimes and also to monitor where police are called to for more serious crimes, a second major innovation was introduced to policing. This involved the building of information gathering systems, often referred to as CompStat programs, which monitored the distribution, in time and space, of criminal action and minor delinquency (Willis, Mastrofski, and Weisburd 2003). CompStat programs became important analytical tools for police agencies to determine how their actions influenced crime, moving them to use the resources gained from freeing themselves up from the constraints of 911 systems to a redeployment to areas in need of the most help. Most importantly, it taught police that, when concentrating their attention on problem areas, they had to follow up on issues that seemed resistant to intervention. Though still based on reactions to crime occurrences, this approach gave policing agencies the chance to adopt some elements of risk management that helped define, albeit on a short time horizon, how police resources were to be managed.

Again, at the time that these changes were being implemented in police organizations, there was only fleeting awareness among criminologists regarding how these changes might affect their views of criminal action, as they continued to see crime problems as a function of vulnerability and offender motivation rather than as a result of the interaction between directed intervention and aggregation of risk. It was less an absence of capable guardians than the selected presence of these guardians (the police) that began to change the ways in which crime patterns developed. As the police moved to a more active role in seeking out risks and tracking them over time, the effectiveness of police interventions improved (even though the organizations remained predominantly responsive, a point we will discuss in the last chapter when we talk about the need to expand the use of more rigorous risk assessment in policing). Further, while it is true that for crime to occur there is a need for an offender and a victim, they do not come together without some form of risk assessment figuring into the equation. Certain factors increase or decrease the likelihood of offender motivation, for example, just as certain factors increase or decrease victims' vulnerability. In our view, failing to recognize the centrality of risk assessment from the criminological view leaves us with an incomplete picture of why crime occurs and how it can be prevented.

CALCULATING SOCIETAL RISK

Risk also has a more societal and global aspect. Efforts have been directed at creating legislation to reduce the likelihood of crime. The European Institute for Crime Prevention and Control, for example, undertook a study to "reduce the probability that an economic/financial/organised crime [would occur] due to opportunities arising from legislation."[8] Further, the probability of crime is reduced by enforcing product codes that require manufacturers to sell electronic goods that are hard to steal. This "crime proofing" assumes that, by changing the characteristics of consumer goods with crime risk in mind, less theft will occur.

We also have examples of the ways in which private sector security operations address the threats that exist while conducting business on a global scale. In an annual effort to update their employees and clients about the risks to the corporation on an international level, CISCO Systems, the world's largest provider of Internet technology, produces a widely distributed document outlining the problems that they face. In a recent report, the authors point to seven major threats to security (primarily related to cybercrime but also to issues related to global business). The first threat, vulnerability of the Internet, addresses the concerns about the extent to which cyber-attacks of all sorts are increasing in number. The resources needed to respond to these threats put heavy strains on companies and their security staff.

The second threat relates to physical assets. Companies have an increased chance of crime and greater difficulties protecting their infrastructure as their global reach increases and as the abilities of local authorities to protect them are limited. This problem is exacerbated by the costs to develop improved facility access control and to develop means to counter vandalism and terrorism threats.

The third threat that is identified resides in the area of legal protection. If this is lacking in certain locations, criminals may operate without punishment and may be involved in corrupt practices that threaten a corporation's business. This connects to the fourth threat, trust, where the concern relates to the degree that companies can rely on their own employees to act legally and in the best interests of the company. The greatest risk to a company's business is from those on the inside.

The fifth threat comes from the need to protect identities, in particular, the information about clients and employees. Identity theft is an increasing concern and has become a key source of risk for companies and individuals operating in cyberspace. Sixth, the report focuses on the threats that are created because of human error—mistakes that increase the risk to a company through the opening of breaches in computer systems, the theft of computers with key information, and so on. Finally, the report says that companies need to be aware of the threats posed by geopolitical conflict. Obviously, areas experiencing social and economic upheaval pose greater risks to companies and their employees.

This report illustrates the new thinking in corporations about crime and other forms of risk that are posed in doing business, domestically and internationally. The challenges in meeting these types of threats set up new requirements within these companies and heavily influence both how they do business and the expectations they place on governments and law enforcement agencies to provide them with protection and support in their efforts to mitigate these risks.

A FRAMEWORK OF THE THREE STAGES OF RISK

In examining crime from a risk perspective, we are cognizant of the many different factors we need to examine to see how probabilities, propensities, and likelihoods connect the important factors used to combat and control crime. We have identified three major facets of risk assessment where the risk dynamic relates to these different dimensions of risk (see table 1.1). First, we identify the nature of the hazard under consideration and whether it constitutes a threat (suggesting impending or potential harm) or an actual danger today. Second, we consider the level of analysis (individual, institutional, or state) associated with the threat being considered. As we have discussed, we acknowledge that people and institutions face threats and hazards that are sometimes abstract and indirect in addition to those that are very specific and easy to identify. These more abstract threats may result in free-floating anxiety that can cause harm. The uncertainty creates challenges at all levels of society as the efforts to prevent abstract harm can be costly and are often hard to justify if the threat is undefined or indeterminate. On the other hand, when facing specific hazards, our framework accounts for the ways in which we prepare for, respond to, and recover from these incidents.

Table 1.1. Risk in Crime Matrix

Stage	Nature of Threat/Hazard	Level of Analysis	Example
	General/Abstract Threat	State	Surveillance
		Institution	Quality of Life Policing
1. Precursor		Individual	Fear
	Specific Hazard	State	Public Security
		Institution	Situational Crime Prevention
		Individual	Criminal Careers
	General/Abstract Threat	State	Crime Waves
		Institution	Managing Threat Information
2. Transaction		Individual	Multiple Victimization
	Hazard	State	Crime Rates
		Specific Institution	Hot Spots
		Individual	Scripts
	General/Abstract Threat	State	Crime Trends and Statistics
3. Aftermath		Institution	CompStat/Punishment
		Individual	Hate Crime
	Specific Hazard	State	Border Control
		Institution	Sex Offender Registries
		Individual	Domestic Violence

On a third dimension we offer a spectrum that runs from the precursors of crime to the incident and then to the aftermath (a process described in detail by Sacco and Kennedy 2002). As Vince Sacco and Leslie Kennedy (2002) make clear, crime explanations can accommodate different factors, and the importance of each explanation depends on what stage of the criminal event is under consideration. The event perspective allows us to tie different components together to explain individual, group, and institutional influences and impacts on crime. The criminal event perspective reminds us to anticipate the effects of motivation, vulnerability, and prevention on crime. From an event perspective, what is left implicit is the likelihood of an event beginning, continuing, and ending in a certain way.

This three-dimensional framework or matrix serves as an organizational tool for the discussions that follow: we locate crime concepts that draw on the notion of risk and demonstrate, through examples, how they can be used to explain the different types of issues that are relevant at these various dimensions. The examples on the right-hand side of table 1.1 are used to illustrate how risk comes into play as suggested by the three dimensions of risk under consideration.

Part of the dilemma in our understanding of crime comes from the imprecision in our understanding of complex systems that we encounter and that actions based on individual decision making, institutional practice, and state-level policies have important impacts on the other levels. In fact, the processing and understanding of risk at these different levels may actually come into conflict with one another. This reality means going beyond simple or single factor solutions. Rather, it requires that we think probabilistically as we face uncertainty and that we learn from the effects of our decisions as we set out to cope with what may be threatening and disorganized environments. As Paul Slovic (2000) observes, "Uncertainty about facts and uncertainty about values both imply that determining the acceptability of a hazard must be an iterative process, partly because, as time goes on, we learn more about how a hazard behaves and how much we like or dislike consequences" (135). The bottom line is that we learn about managing risk through trial and error.

From this matrix, we can see how the concept of risk is central to our thinking about crime in a variety of ways: as surveillance, quality of life policing, fear, scripts, sex offender registries, border control, and so on. The wide array of risk-related concepts shows how deeply embedded these ideas are in our thinking about crime. Yet, relatively little effort has been made to sort out the different meanings of risk and their importance for analyzing criminal events. Our task here is to begin this process. We will order the material to be covered in the next three chapters to examine aspects of our framework, taking each stage of crime risk into consideration. We begin in chapter 2 with the analysis of precursors to crime. In this chapter we consider topics as broad as surveillance and target hardening. In chapter 3, we examine how risk is embedded in the incident itself. How does the notion of risk influence the interaction between the protagonists, and how does context affect the way in which situations create opportunities for crime? In chapter 4, we look at the aftermath of crime. This includes the governance issues that revolve around punishment, deterrence, and revictimization, and the impact this has for future occurrences of crime. In chapter 5, we examine how risk analysis can be used to combine criminological theories through an integrated approach that draws upon our matrix. Chapter 5 also offers an application of risk assessment that makes use of the risk concepts in a practical application for policing.

SUMMING UP

In presenting our model, we suggest that the concept of risk operates at all levels of criminological analysis and changes its character depending on whether or not we look at it before, during, or after the crime incident. In addition, depending on the level of analysis (individual, institution, or state), we will see that risk analysis has been used in different ways to identify, control, respond to, or prevent crime. In the examples we present, we can see that we are often confronted with uncertainty about how and why crime occurs, but risk models provide tools for monitoring through surveillance and direct identification of hazards that can lead to bad outcomes. There is, in addition, a realization that stems from a risk perspective: risk can never be zero. There is always a chance that bad things will happen, and despite all good efforts to take crime down to new lows, we are confronted with the ongoing reality that we will always be facing crime of some sort.

Our discussion emphasizes, however, that the confusion that derives from a myriad of explanations and prescriptions about crime can be reduced somewhat when we draw in the common elements of risk. Understanding that we use risk ideas in different ways, in different contexts (we take risks, we lead risky lifestyles, and we measure risks), there is still a common theme that goes through our analysis when approaching crime problems in this way. Risk, as we have said, provides a metric (albeit influenced by both subjective and objective factors) that can help us tie different parts of the crime problem together. It offers a probabilistic interpretation to crime analysis that allows us to suggest that certain things are likely to happen and others can be prevented based on our risk assessments. It provides a framework, a common structure to our approach that has been missing in previous work on crime. It also makes sense to all of the participants. Offenders know they take risks (and talk about them in explaining their behavior); victims understand they need to reduce risks and insure themselves against them; and police consider risks in doing their jobs but also in understanding how certain areas and certain behaviors can be considered riskier than others.

There is a common script (if not a complete language) that can govern our study of this problem. It is also the case, as we will demonstrate, that criminologists have spoken about and understand risk as an element of crime. Interestingly enough, in their discussions of risk, these analysts have tended to treat risk lightly, rarely incorporating it explicitly into their studies of motivation, opportunity, or prevention (although, of course, a large part of the field is attuned to the ideas of risky lifestyles and rational choices based on risk). We highlight concepts that have considered risk to show how it fits into our larger framework including consideration of offenders, victims, and police. We, of course, go further to show how these theories, concepts, and examples contribute in different ways to a larger risk model that can be used to study crime. Our intent is to begin to break down some of the barriers to communication across the discipline that has prevented a more integrated, contextual approach to crime through an elaboration based on risk.

NOTES

1. Dan Blank, "Reducing the Risk of Crime in Your Store," Expert Business Source, February 25, 2007, at www.expertbusinesssource.com/article/CA6419428.html (accessed April 2008).

2. PA News, "High-Risk Offenders Crime Rises," Channel 4 News, October 22, 2007, at www.channel4.com/news/articles/uk/highrisk+offenders+crime+rises/9465 47 (accessed July 2008).

3. This study can also be found at www.crimereduction.homeoffice.gov.uk/youth/youth63.htm (accessed July 2008).

4. Ken R. Pence, "Rate Your Risk: Evaluate Risks in Your Life," 1995, at www.rateyourrisk.org/ (accessed July 2008).

5. This quotation and study can also be found at http://cjr.sagepub.com/cgi/content/abstract/19/1/56 (accessed July 2008).

6. United Kingdom Home Office, "Crime Reduction: Providing Information and Resources for People Working to Reduce Crime in Their Local Area," at www.crime reduction.homeoffice.gov.uk (accessed July 2008).

7. United Kingdom Home Office, "Safer Schools and Hospitals," April 15, 2005, at www.crimereduction.homeoffice.gov.uk/toolkits/ssh04.htm (accessed July 2008).

8. European Institute for Crime Prevention and Control, "Developing Mechanisms for Assessing the Risk of Crime Due to Legislation and Products in Order to Proof Them against Crime at an EU Level (MARC)," at www.heuni.fi/36851.htm (accessed July 2008).

2

Risk and Precursors to Crime

As we indicated in chapter 1, risk implies uncertainty. When it comes to crime, we cannot be sure of when or where it is likely to happen. We cannot plan for all contingencies. We are not sure where all the threats lie, nor can we say when offenders will strike. We have to plan our responses based on current circumstances, as well as previous experience and knowledge of the contexts that could potentially lead to criminal outcomes. Because we don't know what is certain to happen, we apply strategies that attempt to anticipate bad events or to detect them quickly when they happen so we can move to apprehend offenders and assist victims. We also hope that we will be able to deter offenders, not only if we anticipate correctly where they will act, but also based on offenders' own understanding that they will be identified and detained. The concept of risk involves consideration of particular futures. Because the future is not guaranteed and is uncertain, we attempt to increase the relative degree of certainty through various techniques and behaviors in anticipation of what might be and what we want to have happen. Anticipating and preparing for what might be provides a sense of control. We see that the acceptance of uncertainty as basic to dealing with risk underpins the general argument for passive surveillance that has been made, most specifically in support of the use of closed-circuit television (CCTV) cameras to watch over broad areas of the urban landscape. We begin our discussion of the precursors to crime by examining the experience with CCTV and its successes and failures in mitigating the risk of crime.

SURVEILLANCE (GENERAL/STATE)

The cameras were first installed in town centers on the high streets in major English cities in the mid-1980s during a time of increasing public disorder and theft. Coupled with the growth of in-home security devices, the British public pressed officials for a directed campaign to detect and thwart what they saw as an epidemic of property crime. Since then, the installation of closed-circuit television (CCTV) in public places has continued unabated throughout the United Kingdom in shopping areas, transit stations, buses, airports, parking garages—almost anywhere that people congregate. The full extent of these placements has been brought to public attention in recent times with the use of cameras to solve important crimes that have made the news. The case of the notorious slaying of a young child by two ten-year-olds after he was abducted from a shopping mall was broken open by the surveillance tapes of the shopping mall's parking lot that showed the young boy being led off by the hand by his future assailants. Also, in the case of the London bombings of the Underground in 2005, the suicide bombers were caught on tape entering the station carrying backpacks laden with the ingredients for bombs.

These cases (and many others) have encouraged the authorities to look carefully at the merits of CCTV and its deployment as a tool in discouraging crime and in helping with the apprehension of offenders. In a report prepared in 2007, it is claimed that in London alone there are ten thousand crime-fighting security cameras that cost close to two hundred million British pounds (about 350 million U.S. dollars; Davenport 2007). Clive Norris (2007) has estimated that, in the early 2000s, there were over four million cameras in the United Kingdom costing over a billion dollars (see also McCahill and Norris 2003). This camera proliferation is not restricted to the United Kingdom. There is an estimate that in Times Square alone in New York City over five hundred cameras are operating, raising concerns about not only cost but also the civil liberties of those who work, shop, or go to entertainment in this area whose privacy is compromised by the ubiquitous presence of the cameras (New York Civil Liberties Union 2006).

Despite the very large costs of the fairly extensive net cast by cameras (where each one deployed covers a fairly limited territory and, therefore, needs to be supplemented by others distributed widely and in large numbers), many jurisdictions in North America are now studying ways in which cameras (including cameras attached to police vehicles) can be effectively integrated into crime-prevention strategies. In a recent case in Newark, New Jersey, where three teens were killed execution style in a playground, there was a heated public debate about the fact that the surveillance cameras in this area were not functioning. Operating on the assumption that had they been working this type of crime may have been deterred, the city of Newark developed plans in 2008 to widely deploy working surveillance cameras throughout its neighborhoods.

This CCTV program has an interesting public and private component to it, as well. Many cameras that have been used in criminal cases belong to private businesses that now hand their records over to the police when a crime occurs. With the proliferation of this technological innovation, though, questions remain unanswered concerning the effectiveness of CCTV in deterring or preventing crime. Despite the well-documented cases where camera records have helped in solving crimes, how often is it the case that the camera catches an image that can be decisive in making an arrest?

Before we address this question, it would be useful to put the surveillance issue into risk terms. Where does it fit as a tactic in assessing threats? To fully understand surveillance in these terms, it is apparent that the only thing that really is targeted is a general location in which crime might occur. So, some determination must be made that the camera pointing in a particular direction may help to discourage someone from committing a crime due to fear of being caught. The camera image increases the likelihood of being caught—presumably a negative outcome for the offender—and therefore increases the risk associated with such action. Yet, with all of the cameras being deployed, are they actually focusing on individual threats or is the focus on a more uncertain target? Also, it is clear that the cameras cannot be continuously monitored—there are just too many to be tracked on a real-time basis. The offender would have the advantage in knowing that, while his or her actions are being documented, the police would still have to obtain an ID and find the perpetrator. But, the police and the public are convinced of the cameras' value, and this is partly due to a shift in the ways in which we view risk management despite a claim from the United Kingdom that, in fact, only about 20 percent of the crimes that are captured on camera actually lead to an arrest (Davenport 2007).

The cameras, in many ways, are viewed as the guardians that have been absent in the past and that can be strategically located in areas assumed to be more hazardous, depending on certain characteristics these areas share (not necessarily past history of offending). This can include targeting areas of high transience, areas that concentrate targets, and locations in which local guardianship is less likely to occur (i.e., due to negative neighborhood characteristics). Cameras, then, are allocated according to a risk assessment of areas and targets, an assessment as to where crimes are more likely to occur, and are not assigned to deal with specific threats. Cameras, for example, cannot track offenders but, rather, track geographic space. They attempt to address the uncertainty of offending, a steady sentinel ready to capture the image of a transgression, but cannot be deployed in a way that suggests fore-knowledge that where the camera is aimed will be the place where a crime actually occurs.

This generalized hazard model is consistent with the concept of risk society, popularized in criminology by Richard Ericson and Kevin Haggerty (1997). A crucial shift has taken place in the last few years, they argue, in the ways in which police do their jobs. Instead of focusing on case by case, dealing with the individual differences that each incident brings, police have moved to a strategy that uses surveillance, order maintenance, and prevention to target certain groups of people. The "actuarial" approach, they argue, moves the police to be less concerned about the specific causes of crime and to be more interested in the category of the population that is more likely to offend. This, then, brings surveillance to bear on the areas that these individuals are more likely to frequent. In their assessment of this approach, critics such as Ericson and Haggerty suggest that it brings unfair attention to individuals who are doing no harm within these areas. It also concentrates greater attention on those who belong to minority groups or who are more likely to frequent public spaces. Further, with the extension of the surveillance beyond these areas to a broader saturation of neighborhoods, the reach of the police is extended, and their role changes from deterring crime through their physical presence and solving crime to order maintenance (though some would counter that order maintenance is an integral part of crime control; see our discussion later in this chapter).

An example of surveillance in the face of uncertainty has occurred in New York City where the police conduct random searches of bags and backpacks of individuals entering the subway. When this practice began in the last few years, concerns were raised about the criteria that the police were using to target those who would be searched (the issue is which passengers would be let through since there was no publicly stated, clear set of criteria: searching everyone would be too daunting a task and would slow the movement of people into the subway to a halt). The police have not revealed what would make them suspicious and, therefore, justify a search. The response of the police to the criticism of their tactics is that people can choose to walk away and not be searched. On one hand, this suggests a degree of choice regarding transportation that some passengers simply do not have. On the other hand, it would seem likely that, if someone decided to walk away, this would raise them to a level of suspicion that would prompt the police to search them anyway, arguing that walking away gave them probable cause to do so. In this example, there is no identifiable threat or specific offender, but there is a general acknowledgment that danger exists. Given the perceived general danger, a risk management strategy that promotes surveillance and random searches in order to reduce the probability of negative outcomes is deemed warranted.

But, how effective are these strategies? It is difficult to determine whether or not searching backpacks in a random fashion has deterred any suicide bombers from attacking the New York subway system except to say that at this writing no attacks have occurred. In addition, the police may have available to them information suggesting that attacks might have occurred had the searches not set up a formidable barrier to the potential attackers thereby ensuring that the offenders chose not to act. This does not seem likely as the police seem quick to point out their success in detecting just such a conspiracy, if only to continue to justify their strategies. The searches can also be seen as a means for the police to remind the public to be vigilant about their surroundings and to provide the public with assurances that the police are actively pursuing terrorist threats.

These concerns about the overreach of the law have been expressed about street crime surveillance, but increasingly they are also making their way into the actions of police who have been recruited in counterterrorism efforts. As we said above, random scrutiny of public behavior, either electronically or through direct intervention, has raised worries among privacy advocates and police watchdogs. The surveillance that has taken place on phone calls made to and from suspected terrorists that were conducted by police without the use of warrants (where an argument has been made to a judge that there is reasonable cause to believe that a crime is occurring or is imminent) has generated a great deal of debate about this practice. In its defense, the U.S. government has argued that the suspicion of terrorist activity picked up in these surveillance methods needs to be acted on right away and cannot wait vetting by a judge. The generalized risk, they maintain, makes the cost of not following due process worth it (see Starks [2008] for a discussion of how Congress sought to resolve this conflict in legislation passed in the summer of 2008).

The problem that arises in this case relates to the laws that protect American citizens from investigation by law enforcement without the approval of judges (the government's position related to the telephone calls is that, while domestic communication is protected from this form of warrantless search, any communication with international persons by an American falls outside the restrictions imposed by the law). But, as Susan Kuchinskas (2008) points out in an article published in *Internetnews.com*, the issue concerning privacy goes beyond the individual case. She says that, if the technology that is now used to screen for suspicious calls to "dirty numbers" (numbers connected to known terrorist suspects; Risen and Lichtblau 2005) is not controlled by the telephone companies to identify these suspicious calls but is rather, as some analysts suspect, under the control of government agencies, technical safeguards that are put in place to guard against excessive law enforcement scrutiny can be circumvented. This is not to suggest that abuses are occurring through this surveillance, only that abuse is possible, particularly as there is no clear scrutiny from the judiciary to ensure this does not take place. The potential harm to individual freedom in the face of uncertain threats provides the context in which this debate continues.

Back to the effectiveness of these approaches in the broader realm of surveillance; what does the evidence show? With regard to the implementation of general surveillance strategies, little research has been done to assess its viability (see the review on the empirical evaluation of counterterrorism programs that include surveillance by Cynthia Lum, Leslie Kennedy, and Alison Sherley [2006]). There has been more comprehensive research on the effectiveness of CCTV, particularly in the United Kingdom. Brandon Welsh and David Farrington (2003) have conducted a meta-analysis of all of the available evaluations of the efficacy of CCTV. These evaluations are based primarily on a comparison of the crime that is committed in areas in which CCTV is placed versus areas where the cameras are absent. The locations are matched on the characteristics of the types of people who use these areas and the nature of the land use (car parks, transit, or neighborhoods).

Welsh and Farrington found in the studies that they compared, looking at statistical effects on crime differences, that the only areas in which CCTV are seen to have a direct impact on crime abatement are car parks (i.e., parking garages). They found that those installations with camera surveillance had statistically lower rates of offenses than those without. Now, this research is based on fairly crude measurement and does not take into account solution rates (arrests after the fact), but it provides mixed evidence that CCTV deters crime. Given these weak results, why is there such a strong impetus, as we discussed above, to continue to place cameras all over in town centers, shopping malls, schools, and nearly any other place that people gather?

Part of the answer to this again relates to uncertainty. When we set out to deter crime, because of the complexity of social relations, we are only vaguely aware of what is expected to happen and where we would expect it to happen. Generally, we assume that crime will occur in areas where people congregate and where there are things to steal. Placement of the cameras that provide surveillance of these types of areas suggests to potential offenders (and victims) that someone is invested in making crimes more difficult and also that when the crime occurs there is increased likelihood of detection, pursuit, arrest, and successful prosecution. Now, while the statistics do not support this (remember the results reported from the studies on solution rates from cameras in London, sitting around 20 percent), in the vacuum created by uncertainty, passive surveillance provides some solace to those concerned about their safety and the security of their possessions. The assurances come from the view that somebody is doing something to address the threats (albeit in an undirected and passive way).

There is more to this, of course. Surveillance technology, despite concerns about its encroachment on privacy, has provided dramatic visualization of crimes that have taken place already, searing into the minds of the public the sense of being there when the crime occurred. The images of the toddler led off to his death by two young English boys out of the range of the camera fixed the public mind on the certainty, after the fact, of who the offenders were and the circumstances under which the crime occurred (without providing any plausible explanation as to the reasons for them to behave in the way that they did). Similarly, with the images of the transit bombers laden down with heavy backpacks heading into subway stations, the British public was able to catch a glimpse of the men who turned suicide bombers. This provided a public looking for an understanding of why these crimes would occur with an image of who would take on such a terrible plot. The police, using these images, are also able to say that they can use surveillance as an investigatory tool in solving crimes, and these two examples provide ample evidence to the public that they are right. But, of course, a skeptic would also be right in saying that the crimes occurred despite the presence of the cameras. In the first instance, the young kidnappers were oblivious to their presence and, by their own admission, were not really intending to kill the toddler, and so deterrence of an unplanned crime is really nonsensical. The suicide bombers, of course, had no intention of being caught.

The struggle to deal with uncertainty is matched, then, with the rather imprecise nature of surveillance and the negative consequences that may come from the constant watching of all behavior, not just that which is deemed criminal. Is this overreach of surveillance worth the cost in privacy terms? Advocates of CCTV (and there are many) argue that you needn't be concerned about surveillance if you are not doing anything considered harmful or criminal. The social control that comes from what the critics would call "prying" into private lives of people not engaged in illicit activities is argued not worthwhile.

There is an additional consideration that comes from this surveillance issue. Increasingly, as we pointed out in the example of Newark, cameras and surveillance devices not only are deployed in public areas of commerce (around shopping malls) and transportation (transit stations, airports, and train stations) but also are working their way into neighborhoods. In this expansion, cameras were first located in schools and around school property, but now they are being placed on street corners, in parks, and around housing projects. As planners determine the areas characterized by factors identified as increasing the likelihood of crime, they move the cameras into areas in which there is the greatest amount of crime. In many instances, these locations consist of poor, minority populations who, while they are more likely to be victims of crime and to express a greater need for policing, are also more likely to be subject to remote surveillance of all of their activities in both public and semiprivate locations in ways that do not occur in more affluent areas (and would not be accepted in these locations). The outcome of this reach of surveillance is not yet clear, but if instances occur where the information drawn from this type of oversight is seen as being misused by the police or other public agencies, a whole new debate will open about whether or not this type of control is appropriate (or even legal)—see again the discussion by Ericson and Haggerty (1997).

Our discussion of surveillance highlights how there are abstract threats that impact on perceptions of the likelihood of crime. While CCTV is geared toward specific places—cameras are aimed at and located in particular areas—this method can only address abstractions such as particular categories of people who might offend. Similarly, random checks (if they are, in fact, random) are not used to identify specific offenders but rather address the location—a subway—as being the type of site in which these abstract threats may be realized.

QUALITY OF LIFE POLICING (GENERAL/INSTITUTION)

The observation has often been made that if you leave a building abandoned it will not take very long before a window is broken. Then, quickly thereafter, successive windows will be broken until soon all the windows are destroyed. The message transmitted by the fact that no one has made the effort to fix the first window suggests that no one will stop further damage. Soon, it is maintained, all of the windows disappear and the building becomes derelict. It is this broken windows metaphor that has formed the basis for what is called "quality of life" policing that has become popular across North America, popularized by the successes in crime reduction that accompanied this strategy under the leadership of Chief William Bratton in New York City. This form of policing emphasizes an approach that targets minor crime as a way of deterring or detecting more serious crime. The challenges that were faced in implementing this approach are well chronicled in books by Bratton (Bratton and Knobler 1998) and George Kelling and Catherine Coles (1996). Bratton and Kelling (2006) point to the real successes that have derived from the application of broken windows approaches to crime prevention. For example, the large decreases in crime rates observed in Los Angeles after its implementation in 2002 were credited to this approach.

The broken windows policing approach has been criticized for its apparent disregard for the civil liberties of people involved in minor disorder offenses in its broad targeting of offenders. Further, it has been criticized for its promotion of arrest over other strategies. Yet, while criticized for emphasizing zero tolerance, this strategy is not central to broken windows policing—nor does the perspective promote indiscriminate arrests.

The debate continues to rage back and forth over the merits of the approach based on the successes it has produced, while its limitations are chronicled in the research results that appear to deny its claims of effectiveness. Further critiques of this approach appear in studies by Ralph Taylor (2000) and Robert Sampson and Stephen Raudenbush (1999). These critics maintain that a central thesis in this approach, that social disorder threatens quality of life and is connected to crime outcomes, is not supportable in research findings. Jacinta Gau and Travis Pratt (2008) go even further to state that disorder and crime are indistinguishable to residents, so the basic premise that disorder causes crime is not supportable. This point could be seen as a major flaw in this approach if we were to test its merits on the exactness with which police tactics responded to crime. However, as Bratton and Kelling (2006) argue, broken windows theory has never suggested that there is a direct link between social decay and crime. Rather, "from the first presentation of broken windows we have argued, to the contrary, that the link, while clear and strong, is *indirect*. Citizen fear, created by disorder, leads to weakened social controls, thus creating the conditions in which crime can flourish."

However, establishing the link between social disorder and crime is not really the point of this approach in the first place (hence the response by Bratton and Kelling that the proof of the approach rests with the effectiveness of the results, notwithstanding the lack of clarity in the research findings). In fact, the critics and the proponents of this approach may actually be talking past one another. In support of this approach, police officers, as quoted by Kelling and Coles (1996), maintain that going after petty offenses will have the effect of keeping those individuals from committing more serious offenses. In addition, the order-maintenance outcomes are such that the community is less intimidated and becomes more involved in dealing with the crime problem. It is therefore the reduction of the perceived likelihood of crime, interpreted by the actors in an environment as defined by their levels of fear, rather than the objective characteristics of social decay, per se, that is important as this obviously derives from an emphasis on how people judge the negative effects of social disorder. This point is supported by Gau and Pratt (2008) who conclude that it is not the incivility or disorders themselves that cause crime but rather the social construction of this disorder that is important. In other words, if people see the disorder but don't care about it, it has no effect. If they see the disorder and this triggers fear or aversion, then the effect is real.

The debate about the strengths and weaknesses of this approach will go on for a long time as it is not only a disagreement over tactics but also a disagreement over the role that the police should play in maintaining order. Without engaging further in the merits of this debate, let's take a look at the broken windows approach from a view that takes risk into account and see what it has to say about how crime might emerge from conditions of social disorder. As discussed earlier concerning the rationale behind surveillance strategies, in explaining the precursors to crime, we confront a great deal of uncertainty about threats to our safety. In confronting this uncertainty, a determined effort is made by police to identify particular dangers—most often based on previous experience and patterns of crime. But, when there is a great deal of crime, this type of targeted response may be less effective. As was the case in the mid-1980s, there was an emergent problem of crime where police had difficulty keeping up with offenders and crime rates kept growing. What seemed called for was a strategy that dealt less with the probability of a specific crime occurrence and more, instead, with the general exposure to crime that comes from proximity to offenders and concentration of opportunities (both in terms of victims and their property). Broken windows approaches sought to focus on areas where offenders could operate freely and where victims might be easy targets. The strategy was not to catch offenders in the act but rather to remove them long before they could commit a serious offense and to embolden the people in the community to increase their collective sense of self-protection. The self-fulfilling nature of the disorder then was turned upside down to become a self-fulfilling sense of order. This idea of self-fulfilling prophecies and crime is discussed as an example of a "tipping point" where, left unattended, crime will take over a neighborhood simply because offenders are numerous and those who can or are able to fight against this crime either give up or leave (see Gladwell 2000). The sense of added risk of harm in an area contributes to the movement toward the tipping point so that, once individuals feel they are no longer secure, there is a collapse in the social order of the community.

If steps are taken to avoid reaching this tipping point (which by its very nature is dynamic), the uncertainty of crime is replaced with a certainty of safety. So, from a risk perspective, whether or not arresting minor offenders specifically keeps them from committing more serious crime can be proven is not really the point. The point is that, by dealing with the general threat of crime through diminishing the threats associated with disorder, overall crime problems diminish. Added to this (although this has been offered as a critique of broken windows but can really, from a risk perspective, be seen as complementary), the reduction of the probability of crime (or perceived probability of crime) through collective action can have an important effect on whether or not the community is able to recover. The idea of collective efficacy suggests that the inhabitants can come together to defeat the negative effects of social disorder (Sampson and Raudenbush 1999). They do this through increased resistance to negative influences, demanding greater support from police and focusing on support of victims. Now, it may be true that safety is an illusion. Crime may still continue. But, the calculation of the perceived likelihood of crime is altered. Areas that previously were seen as uninhabitable become newly renovated neighborhoods; people make investments in houses and schools. The community develops new expectations about what the police can do to keep areas safe and free of crime. As Wesley Skogan (2008) argues, what people in distressed neighborhoods want from the police, when they meet to discuss steps that can be taken to address problems, is an effort to clean up neighborhoods both in terms of incivilities and physical decay. Down the list of concerns expressed are problems of crime. This is not to say that crime is unimportant or that disorder is not part of crime, but it does point to the concerns about how residents perceive the chances of crime. If the efforts to clean up areas are successful, the need for quality of life policing would recede as the risks of crime become more clearly specified and understood. People who are more likely to follow the rules will expect less intervention from police in their daily lives and will not see much opportunity to act with respect to noncriminal order maintenance because the community is itself taking care of these problems. But, as uncertainty grows again, there may be once again a call for more of this type of action.

This is underlined in the statements made in 2008 by the Newark, New Jersey, police director Gary McCarthy (a veteran of New York City policing), who suggested that the solution to the new surge in violent crime in the city is to return to quality of life policing. While there is a plan to target offenders who strike out and hurt others, there is a strong belief in the leadership of cities undergoing this type of crime surge that the police need to deal not only with offenders but also with disorder. Again, with greater exposure to the hazards that comes with an apparent rise in crime, patrols that focus on street nuisances like public intoxication, which might be ignored in low-crime periods, can be used to signal to offenders that police are present and willing to act on behavior that is publicly unacceptable. In addition, the police take advantage of their involvement in minor crime control to remove individuals who may become more serious offenders.

Broken windows theories serve as one part of an overall strategy to the effects that social disorganization can have on crime. This approach targets, in particular, the strategies that police need to use to deal with disorder. But it is clear that there is more to this problem than public disorder. In a thought-provoking article written for *New York Magazine*, Chris Mitchell (2008) set out to explore the root causes of crime, specifically investigating the reasons for the steep drop in crime. Mitchell makes the observation that killings in New York City in 2008 had plummeted to new lows. Then he asks, What would it take to get the murder rate to zero? And would the city be better off? The idea that we might see a day when there are less than five hundred murders (the number in 2006 was 921) in a city that, at its peak of violence in 1990, experienced over 2,605 murders a year is weird enough to those who have chronicled the problems of New York at its worst: struggling with poverty, drug use, and stranger violence. But the notion that we would be able to envision a city with no murders in one year seems beyond comprehension, or is it? In his article, Mitchell chronicles a number of possibilities that, combined, might lead the murder rate down further to almost nothing. These solutions reflect a mélange of those discussed above, combining police intervention with social action. His discussion provides an interesting application of ways of addressing the debate about the causal effects of social disorganization on crime. Although Mitchell does not make explicit use of the concept of risk throughout his discussion, the use of this concept would provide greater coherence to his argument. Mitchell's list includes continuing surveillance and more police (reminiscent of broken windows approaches); broader and more assertive domestic violence intervention; legalization of drugs; identification of the motivations of serious offenders; and home ownership. Mitchell's list seems strangely heterogeneous, mixing actions of the authorities with offender propensities and changes in the economic structure of the city. So, how would this disparate collection of factors contribute to violence reduction?

Mitchell argues that the combination of these efforts and the overall success that has been achieved in controlling killings over the past decade might create sufficient momentum to continue this downward trend. But despite past gains, Mitchell hesitates in applying his prescriptions for total abatement, as he admits he is not really sure of the advisability of some strategies, such as individualized assessments of troubled individuals that might lead to drastic measures to incapacitate them (hence his caveat about whether or not the city would be better off). But with the hopefulness of his plans for crime reduction, it is hard to dismiss Mitchell's review and suggestions for action, even though the premise that crime might completely disappear is somewhat fatuous (although it provides an interesting point of departure in trying to understand how crime impacts our lives).

If we were to examine in more detail each of Mitchell's solutions, what are the bases for the belief that these strategies would work? Are there commonalities across these prescriptions that would help explain why we would include each as a factor in crime reduction? First, Mitchell's suggestion of continued monitoring and surveillance to manage crime outcomes makes intuitive sense. For example, if we can identify geographically where a problem is occurring, we are better able to get resources to that location to stop the crime before it occurs or to prevent it from recurring. He advocates increased surveillance and close examination of crime rates as ways of monitoring, responding, and deterring crime. In other words, surveillance and monitoring crime rates are means to address a heightened likelihood of crime happening in particular areas.

Second, connected to this is the idea that success with surveillance and monitoring is possible only if we have adequate numbers of police members to identify and deal with these problems. It has been repeatedly shown that police presence has an impact on crime reduction: police decrease the likelihood of crime by deterring would-be offenders. The problem posed by crime analysts is how much police presence is required to deter criminals from acting? The direct relationship between police deployment and crime occurrence is difficult to quantify, yet through ongoing monitoring there has been real gains in police success in managing this balance over the past few years (see, in particular, the discussions around the successes related to police deployment that derive from computerized auditing systems that track crime occurrences and police response: David Weisburd [2008] refers to this as "place-based policing").

We then must confront the problems that don't respond well to simple surveillance or enhanced police response. Mitchell's second factor relates to the need to legalize drug crimes. He begins by raising a complicated set of questions about the impact that drug use has on urban environments. Legalization might remove the barriers that result due to charges of possession of drugs, but violence that erupts out of drug cultures is connected to not just drug sales but also the consequences of addiction. Illegal drug use has emerged, once again, as a vortex around which a number of other types of crimes and issues emerge. The importation and distribution of drugs has spawned a vast underground criminal enterprise. While the consumers of these drugs are distributed widely throughout urban and suburban areas, the concentration of drug buying, selling, and consumption in distressed inner-city areas has fueled a storm of violence. Gangs fight over turf, individuals rob others for money, and the abuses of prostitution coexist with drug use, providing sustenance for drug habits and bolstering the drug trade. Added to this, we find that these problems more often form in areas where there are no real communities but that are instead populated by dispossessed young males driven from other parts of the city by redevelopment. Past histories of criminal involvement discourage them from living in public housing or returning to their families.

This population may end up in "no man's land," where there is little social control and an absence of police presence. In these situations, self-defense, retaliation, and aggressive behavior prevail. Could drug legalization curtail the violence? Perhaps, but the question remains whether it is the drugs or the desperate lives of the inhabitants of these areas that spawn the violence. Even with legalization, the drug culture would remain (although possibly without the battles over clients that currently drives the violence in these areas and without the stigma of criminalization). Legalization of drugs may decrease the risk of certain types of violence but may not reduce other hazards associated with drug cultures.

But, the outcome of drug legalization vis-à-vis violence cannot be considered without addressing the effects of alcohol. Although legalized, alcohol continues to fuel disputes and is often cited as a major factor in escalating violence to homicide. In addition, it is an important contributor to other serious forms of public safety violations, for example, traffic fatalities. The lesson learned from this is that the legalization of a drug may not remove its negative effects if addiction and violence are not considered. This drugs/alcohol/violence mix is particularly of concern when we consider Mitchell's next point.

Mitchell's third prescription outlines the difficulties faced with the damaging effects of domestic relations that escalate toward violence over a period of tumultuous interactions. Advocates have argued for an assertive form of intervention early in these altercations. For example, the New York Police Department has responded by conducting follow-up visits on incidents in a way that encourages safety among victims and deterrence for offenders, bringing the number of repeat offenses down. Unfortunately, it is the case that, unless reported by others who witness or hear of the incident, many of these attacks do not come to the attention of the police (less than half according to a report by Timothy C. Hart and Callie Rennison [2003] based on findings from the National Crime Victimization Survey). Increasing success in deterring domestic violence, through stronger police action and better detection, would serve as an important ingredient in bringing overall homicide rates lower.

Fourth, Mitchell turns attention to the psyche of the offender who is violent. The idea that there is a "propensity to commit crime" continues to attract attention, although the idea that there is a crime gene that controls criminal behavior does not have much currency in today's crime debates. The diagnostics involving genetic testing that could be used to detect the "born criminal" are not particularly reliable and pose some real ethical dilemmas in their use, as there are likely to be many "false positives"—predicting crime propensity when none exists—in identifying those who may commit illegal acts or become violent. While genetic testing for would-be offenders may not provide the detection hoped for, the idea that offenders can be identified in advance of offending has been a long-standing goal of criminologists.

Fifth, Mitchell presents the idea that home ownership will lower crime. He explains that people who own their own homes will be more committed to providing long-term surveillance, deterring offenders, and assisting others to make their neighborhoods better places to live. There is consistent support for a negative relationship between home ownership and crime. The caution in this tale is the exclusionary nature of building residential areas where those who can't afford to own are pushed into areas that are socially and economically disorganized, becoming dangerous (a point we discussed above).

Together these factors should result in an even lower level of violent crime, Mitchell asserts. His analysis reflects how criminologists have approached questions about what causes crime. The tentativeness with which he approaches the subject may derive from weak evidence of the roots of violence and past experience: just when we think we have a clear understanding of a social problem, it takes on a new life or morphs into something quite different. For example, taking Mitchell's prescription at face value, assuming that this is more of an explanation for the current drop than an explanation for a future one, how do we account for the rather disjointed and unrelated set of solutions that are offered here? Further, is it reasonable to assume that crime will ever completely go away? And, if it continues to stay low, are we even sure why it stays low and does not go back up? We would like to find a common thread that runs through these explanations that helps us make sense of why crime rises or drops and what we can do about it. As it stands, the solutions are set alone, with no underlying rationale that connects them other than the specific effects that each are expected to have on crime outcomes.

So, while Mitchell's analysis is interesting and the challenge to find the prescription for a zero homicide rate a compelling one, his treatise fails to convince without identifying the common thread running among his points. We are left without a clear understanding of why these prescriptions would work or not and what they have to do with one another. There is no real account of the ways in which individuals and agencies make choices or how different factors influence their decision making. What is missing in this approach, we believe, is an assessment of the risk that underpins criminal behavior and its control. Surveillance and monitoring, for example, are specifically about reducing the likelihood of crime. Similarly, intervening in difficult interpersonal relationships is thought to reduce the probability of violent events occurring. Determination of individual "crime propensity" also relates to lowering probabilities that potential offenders may offend—through early detection and, presumably, incapacitation. So what's new about this approach using risk as a unifying theme? Depending upon one's perspective, assessments of risk may

create opportunities to commit crime (offenders consider the likelihood of being caught, for example), at the same time that we know others take measures
to reduce their risk of victimization. Again, how does paying attention to risk
improve on the explanations offered by Mitchell and others in telling us why
crime goes up and down?

As with the broken windows example, we have difficulty quantifying the
impact of interventions or understanding the mechanisms through which they
impact on crime. By focusing on risk, we can articulate the effects of, for
example, more proactive forms of policing and accountability that have been
introduced into modern policing. Further, police can team up with other agencies and with the public to identify innovative ways to reduce the likelihood
of crime and to control its outbreak, including direct intervention in domestic
violence, proactive efforts at fighting drug culture violence, and efforts to
include the community in crime fighting. Using another example, the lessons learned from the private sector in their approaches to security involving
"enterprise risk management"—making use of methods and processes to
capitalize on opportunities or avoid hazards to meet institutional goals—have
led us to consider how risk influences our explanations of crime origins and
abatement. These are all themes that we will return to as we move through
the different stages of our model of risk.

FEAR (GENERAL/INDIVIDUAL)

As we can see from this discussion of uncertainty and exposure in environments in which crime thrives, a major factor influencing how institutions
respond to these problems is fear. Fear of crime has influenced political cam-
paigns; unseated police chiefs; created massive migrations of people away
from embattled inner cities; created high demand for rapid police response;
and helped form a large security industry built around protecting people and
things from offenders (including, as we stated earlier, the installation of hun-
dreds of thousands of closed-circuit surveillance cameras). In the research
literature that has focused on the bases upon which people develop fear, the
common finding is that fear rises and falls despite apparent actual threats to
safety or experience with crime. Further, fear is more intensely felt among
certain groups, in particular among women and the elderly (Warr 1984). So,
absent immediate threats, why do people report high levels of fear? Jonathan
Jackson (2006) offers an explanation. He says that the "worry about crime"
literature suggests that fear of crime is formed by "an appraisal of threat com-
prising perceptions of likelihood, control, and consequences. In turn, infer-
ences about victimization risk were shaped by beliefs about crime incidence,

and both were largely a product of interpretations of the physical and social environment" (257).

In a sense, then, this approach suggests that it is the reinforcing nature of the external stimulus that people encounter that raises their worry and this, in turn, makes them more attuned to signs of disorder. But there is an alternative explanation that helps explain why individuals who have not been victimized or who live in less disorganized environments may also have increased levels of fear. This derives from what Jackson (2006) refers to as the "psychology of risk" that evokes in individuals images of loss and injury that may be unconnected to actual experience. The cognitive evaluation (or individual accounting) evaluation of risk can exist side by side with the emotional (image of risk) responses. This approach is consistent with the view that individuals develop ways of managing perceived risk (and their emotional expression of fear) based on their perceptions of what is likely to happen, not solely on what they objectively believe to happen. As Jackson states, "Equally, if crime is judged to have severe consequences, and the outcome is vivid and affect-laden, then that individual is likely to be insensitive to probability variations. That individual is unlikely to feel better if he or she is told that the chances of victimization are rather slight" (258). This is probably an overstatement of the risk assessment that individuals undertake; as we will see later in the discussion, the probability of harm cannot be completely discounted in individual levels of fear. It is clear, however, that risk is calculated by individuals in ways that differ from what we would expect (and what experts would predict) based on the actual likelihood of victimization.

In the surveys that have been done across the United States and internationally, when respondents are asked about their fear, in all cases they report that they are afraid of general threats in their immediate neighborhoods, including areas in which there is apparent disorder and areas where groups of young people collect together (Van Dijk et al. 2007). This becomes what has been called "free-floating fear," connected to the uncertainty of all sorts of dangers in the environment. Given this overall concern, is this fear rational or just something that emerges as one of life's anxieties, added to fear of disease, disasters, and accidents? In looking at this from a risk perspective, we can see that fear is actually an orienting device for people to manage their immediate environments both by limiting their exposure to dangers and also through developing mitigating responses, such as reducing opportunities for crime and harm through self-protection.

Concerning the rationality of fear and risk management, Jackson's ideas conform to the work that has been done by risk psychologists to determine how people judge the chances of bad things happening to them. Paul Slovic, who has spent his career studying different aspects of risk in various realms of life, has pointed out that people are often wrong in their estimates of the actual likelihood of problems such as road accidents, homicides, diseases, and the like, occurring. As we mentioned in the previous chapter, and this point is reinforced above, people are influenced by emotions in making judgments about their environments. Fear constitutes an affective response. People make determinations about security in their personal circumstances based on information they hear from others; the connections they make to a particular event they know about; and what they hear from experts. But they also use their own intuition. The ways that people make these judgments of risk have been presented in the work of Amos Tversky and Daniel Kahneman (1981) whose "prospect theory" suggests that these risks are summarized by and reduced to shortcuts, scripts, or "heuristics" that people use to guide them in their daily lives (see also Kahneman and Tversky 1979).

In their explanation of these heuristics, Tversky and Kahneman (1981) report three: representativeness, availability, and anchoring. Representativeness allows individuals to make judgments about hazards and threats based on things they have previous knowledge of, depending on how closely the current experience matches that knowledge. This shortcut can help people figure out what may happen, as it should coincide with what they consider to be a comparable experience. However, when fear levels rise, this shortcut may be derailed by improper comparisons or biases that lead to incorrect judgments about what might happen. For example, the long-standing concern about crime in major urban areas has created a high level of anxiety about the risks that one can encounter when traveling into or out of these locations. This fear can persist even in the face of direct evidence that changes have occurred to reduce the actual chance of becoming a victim.

Also influencing judgments of risk and probabilities of harm and opportunity is a second shortcut that people use to assess risk, the availability heuristic. In this case, people refer to what is known about a certain problem. If there is continued discussion of the frequency of violent crime in a certain location, for example, this will set the standard for deciding on the chances of harm associated with responding in certain ways. Events that occur in large numbers are more influential than those that occur less often, yet the reference points for deciding when the balance has been tipped either in favor of or against a particular outcome is often left indeterminate, leaving biases in the assessments that people make about risk. For example, a city that has had a long experience with crime may be in the process of cleaning up many of its problems, but the perception that negative events are likely to occur remains with those who remember the "bad old days" when many dangers lurked in these areas and people quickly left for safer locales. The rebuilding of the downtown neighborhoods of some of the secondary cities in the United States (cities that have not seen the rebounding confidence experienced by those such as New York, Chicago, Seattle, or San Francisco) has been slowed by this lack of confidence by outsiders (some who live in not-too-distant suburbs) in their ability to maintain safe and secure environments for people to work, live, or find entertainment.

The third heuristic, anchoring, is based on assessing our fear of a particular type of threat. What this means is that people base their judgments only on sensational events ignoring the fact that these events occur rarely and therefore have a limited chance of actually impacting individuals. This could also mean that people who do not know about actual dangers in their environment and focus on the less serious crimes underestimate their risk of victimization, lower their fears, and so operate in ways that may expose them to dangers.

Let's take an example of how these heuristics work. If we were to look at how these shortcuts might connect the fears of the elderly to their judgments of risk we see an interesting story emerging. In terms of representativeness, while the elderly are less likely to be victims of crime, partly because they are less mobile and rarely frequent public places at night, they make assessments of their likely victimization based on what they hear in the media and from friends about the extent of crime that occurs in their surroundings. Crime occurring in and around their homes, even though not directed at them, can be seen as threatening and perceived as increasing their risk of crime. Then, the availability heuristic as it applies to crime against the elderly comes into play. In this case, we see the interesting generalizing effect that fear can have on people.

In a study of elderly respondents, Kennedy and Robert Silverman (1985) reported an intriguing finding where, despite having no experience with crime, elderly living in their own homes expressed higher than expected levels of fear. In making sense of this, Kennedy and Silverman found a suggestive anomaly in the findings. The fear levels in this group were actually heightened in the case of the respondents who had higher levels of contacts with their relatives rather than among those who were more socially isolated. The authors speculated that this higher fear level was a direct result of the warnings of dangers in their locations that the family members directed to their elderly relatives who were living alone in their homes. Of course, this fear would be further enhanced with anchoring stories of individuals who actually were victims of attacks, elderly folks living alone in their homes. While the risk of this type of victimization was in fact low, based on victimization statistics, the resulting fear levels were high.

A few years ago, during a regular survey of the population of Winnipeg, Manitoba, researchers noticed a sudden spike in fear levels among respondents. In trying to make sense of this, they made inquiries of local law enforcement to establish whether or not there had been a sudden rise in crime or an outbreak in violence. The survey respondents appeared to be particularly troubled by the possibility of being victims of the most serious offenses, but the researchers could find no evidence of any of this type of crime occurring at the time in the Winnipeg area. Then, it occurred to someone that, in the months before the survey, the local cable television company had just introduced a new service that included broadcasts of a new American "superchannel" from Detroit. This channel was basically the local channel that included national programming. But, it also included local Detroit news. At the time, there was a great deal of crime on the streets of Detroit, and this was dutifully reported every night on the six o'clock news. Although a thousand miles away from Winnipeg, the reports of these crimes, it was speculated, were the major reason for the increased fear levels witnessed there. Such is the sensitive nature of fear. Even without local anchoring events and acknowledgment that the experiences in Detroit were quite different from what could be witnessed in Winnipeg, the possibilities of danger still prevailed. The greater awareness of the possible risks (however remote) stirred the viewers to respond with fear.

For those who have done research on fear, it would come as no surprise that this type of reaction would develop. After all, there is a consistent and systematic variation across demographic groups in what have become standard measures of fear, the most commonly used measure being fear of walking alone in one's neighborhood at night. Women and the elderly will always report higher levels of concern in response to this question. Now, of course, it is the case that people who have been victimized will be more fearful, but men who have been victims will, on average, still report lower levels of fear than women who have not. When we examine these results, we can see a strong element of consequence that comes from the effects of fear. In viewing their environment, the consideration of risk certainly comes from the heuristics laid out above, but it also comes from a consideration of the consequences that come from taking a risk and becoming a victim. Fear serves as a way of reminding people of what they may suffer as a victim of a crime. As in the case of the elderly, they could stay in their homes alone and do fine, but what would happen if they were attacked? The consequences would be much more severe than for others. But, in response, the elderly might say that, while recognizing the risk of being attacked when alone, the offsetting benefit of having the independence of living alone is worth it.

Given these calculations, how does fear impact on risk calculations? Obviously, with a disconnect between experience and fear levels, the calculus is somewhat loosely made, but the force of feeling fearful is real nonetheless. As Slovic emphasizes, perception is an important factor in determining how people manage risk. And perception is heavily influenced by what it is that people fear. Just as objective elements associated with hazards figure into the calculations of risk, so too do subjective elements. How these factors combine to determine behavior or response may be individually or institutionally specific. The challenge, however, is to identify patterns of responses that characterize these outcomes.

PUBLIC SECURITY (SPECIFIC/STATE)

Since the 2001 attack on the World Trade Center, there has been increased interest in looking at ways to counter the terrorism threat. In much of the literature that has emerged, there has been a strong focus on threatening groups and their tactics that menace and mobilize violence against societies. These groups have been identified as following particular ideologies, through detailed efforts to understand their tactics and their target preferences (Sageman 2004). While there has been some real success in countering the actions of terrorist groups through concentrated intelligence gathering and targeted responses, there is still a large amount of terrorist action that is hard to predict and very general so that specific targets are often hard to identify or protect (as is the case with concerns about protecting mass-transit facilities of major cities, areas that have been preferred targets of past attacks). When we have little knowledge about who might launch an attack or when this might occur, but we are sure that an attack is likely, we find ourselves managing risk in a way that promotes a general form of prevention against all possibilities. But this type of risk management is difficult to sustain and difficult to defend. The major exception are the strategies that were implemented after a rash of plane hijackings in the 1970s requiring that all passengers boarding planes are subject to checks.

In reviewing research on the effectiveness of counterterrorism approaches instituted over the years, Lum, Kennedy, and Sherley (2006) found that empirical evidence for the effectiveness of these efforts is really only available for airport security (and for efforts to protect foreign embassies from bomb attacks). This should not be interpreted as suggesting that airport screening is the only effective way to deter terrorists or hijackers, but it is the only demonstrably effective approach. Part of the reason that airport screening is effective is the extent to which access to the facility is controlled with protocols developed for reducing dangers to travelers and to planes. In the controlled environment of airports, everyone is subjected to a search, and particular objects are targeted that have been deemed threatening (from guns to knives to containers of liquids). The success of these searches (with a few bumps in the road from screenings that miss weapons or allow unticketed individuals past

entry points) is shown in the rapid decline in hijackings after the implementation of metal detectors in airports in the 1970s and the lack of attack on planes
in recent years (after the breach that occurred during 9/11).

Airport security is a form of risk management applied to particular targets—airports and planes. Security checks and metal detectors are put into
place to reduce the likelihood of an unwanted outcome: a terrorist attack.
Ronald Clarke and Graeme Newman (2006) advocate a similar sort of general risk approach by identifying targets that terrorists would see as suitable
to their efforts to attract attention and cause widespread grief. In protecting
these targets, we reduce the likelihood of attack with, presumably, little displacement to other areas: targets become targets because of their suitability as
such—not because they can be easily substituted with other targets. The logic
of this approach, given the difficulty in managing all targets, makes some
sense in the context of limited resources. The issue of displacement is still a
question as we see a migration of attacks from airplanes and major symbolic
buildings, like embassies and the World Trade Center, to harder-to-protect
facilities like transit stations, buses, and nightclubs.

This approach to threats has encouraged counterterrorism authorities to
place their attention on what is referred to as infrastructure protection, a task
that provides a general inventory of possible targets that are then rated for
their likely attack. The U.S. Department of Homeland Security (DHS) has
developed what they call the National Infrastructure Protection Plan (NIPP)
where they outline a plan to protect critical infrastructure and key resources
through a risk mitigation program. In their words,

> The NIPP framework will enable the prioritization of protection initiatives
> and investments across sectors to ensure that government and private sector
> resources are applied where they offer the most benefit for mitigating risk by
> lessening vulnerabilities, deterring threats, and minimizing the consequences
> of terrorist attacks and other manmade and natural disasters. The NIPP risk
> management framework recognizes and builds on existing protective programs
> and initiatives.
>
> Protection includes actions to mitigate the overall risk to CI/KR [Critical In-
> frastructure/Key Resources] assets, systems, networks, functions, or their inter-
> connecting links resulting from exposure, injury, destruction, incapacitation, or
> exploitation. In the context of the NIPP, this includes actions to deter the threat,
> mitigate vulnerabilities, or minimize consequences associated with a terrorist at-
> tack or other incident. . . . Protection can include a wide range of activities, such
> as hardening facilities, building resiliency and redundancy, incorporating hazard
> resistance into initial facility design, initiating active or passive countermea-
> sures, installing security systems, promoting workforce surety programs, and
> implementing cyber security measures, among various others. (DHS 2006, 1)

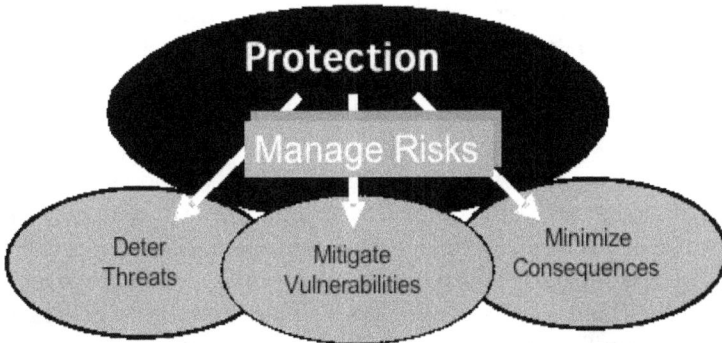

Figure 2.1. Department of Homeland Security Protection Strategy (adapted from Department of Homeland Security. 2006. *National Infrastructure Protection Plan*. Washington, D.C.).

The DHS has compiled a national list of these targets and then ranked them according to their importance and their vulnerability. On the list are chemical plants, transit facilities, utilities, and so on. In managing this ranking, DHS then assigns values to the resources that are needed to protect the higher-ranking targets. This suggests, at least at the national level, there is a general sense that targets might be interchangeable and that the costs and benefits of protection and the consequences of attack can be predetermined and prevention strategies developed for the most important targets (according to this ranking).

Some commentators are critical of this approach as it puts too much emphasis on targets and not enough on the likelihood of attack. Without understanding motivation, it is said, we have little hope of understanding where the next attack might be. Yet, as the airport screening example shows, we can have success in reducing risk (the likelihood of harm) through good prevention strategies without understanding why these facilities become targets in the first place (we may find this out later on and then act accordingly).

Niyazi Ekici and others (2008) shed some light on this issue of target choice through a research project that they conducted involving the Turkish National Police. Turkey has a large number of terrorist attacks, particularly bombings, perpetrated by three major terrorist groups. Ekici and his colleagues asked counterterrorism specialists to rate major targets in Istanbul, using the criteria of high values laid out in the work by Clarke and Newman, who propose that terrorists will select targets based on eight criteria. This includes whether or not these locations are Exposed, Vital, Iconic, Legitimate, Destructible, Occupied, Near, and Easy (EVIL DONE) and that the targets ranked high on these lists have inherent value as targets.

When the police officers completed their ratings, there were some surprises in the results. The raters actually ranked an underground metro station higher on the list of targets for terrorists than two very large and symbolically important buildings (a large bank building and a shopping center) both of which had been previously attacked. When asked to explain their choices, the terror experts suggested that the attack on the transit station offered the most effective way for the terrorists to disrupt daily life. But, as important, the raters suggested that the targets would be selected according to the message that the terror group wanted to send, depending on their ideology. In other words, the attack was not simply meant to attract attention per se but was also seen as a way of communicating the groups' rejection of the political and economic order of the society under attack. When asked why these attacks had not been directed at the metro station to this point, the raters suggested that these locations were heavily patrolled and securely protected against attack, deterring the terrorists from acting. It is clear from this that the police are involved in anticipating where attacks will come. Planned responses to these do not just consider the "suitability" of the target in terms of access or vulnerability but also anticipate that the groups involved in these actions take into account the reaction that these attacks will create in highlighting their ideologies and stated forecast.

It is in determining the latter that difficulties appear in translating terrorists' creeds into action. There is a great deal of guesswork involved in this, particularly as terrorist groups actively pursue new targets in order to evade police detection. In the case of terrorism, the complexity that appears as a result of the crime actually serving as a symbol of some underlying political or social motive makes this form of prevention difficult. All the same, it is true that acknowledging the focus of these groups (as we said, there are three identifiable groups operating in Turkey) makes the anticipation of certain general types, if not specific instances, easier to forecast.

If we return to the general problem of common crime, which is not usually influenced by political messages or ideological statements, prevention strategies may be successful without understanding why an offender might act and may be general enough to deter offenders without dealing with specific threats. An interesting example of this comes from the successes that we have seen in the prevention of car theft. When automobiles became easy targets for both "clouts" (objects stolen from the car) and thefts of the car itself, the police and the auto industry worked on two strategies. One was to go after the demand for cars, in both the illegal market for parts and the market for cars to be resold in foreign locations. But police also concentrated heavily on the task of making the car hard to steal in the first place, encouraging the car industry to build in prevention devices and prodding owners to use them. With the development of advanced locks, kill switches, alarms, and tracking devices, it is increasingly more difficult to steal a car, regardless of the reason for the theft. This form of risk management comes with the vehicle (the proofing that we talked about earlier) and allows only authorized users access. This type of risk management has had the effect of driving car theft down as it is simply more difficult to enter and start newer vehicles today. Clouts, of course, require a different type of response, but theft itself is less likely to occur under these conditions.

In the context of crime, the effort to provide general responses to specific crimes evolves from prevention efforts that encourage people and businesses to develop general practices that reduce their likelihood of crime victimization. As reported in chapter 1, crime-prevention websites give suggestions on how to reduce theft from shops and how to protect one's car from being stolen. These approaches define risk in terms of response. If you are successful in your efforts to protect your goods, you will not be victimized. Basic to these self-help sites is the principle that, just as there are specific means by which crimes can be perpetrated, there are also general rules that can be followed to protect oneself. This learning approach to self-protection works on the assumption that, if people follow general principles of risk management, they will be free of crime.

The United Kingdom Home Office (2008) has demonstrated, though, that general advice on crime prevention should not relate only to protecting property. In 2008, the Home Office initiated a new effort to combat crime that provides for specific attention to be paid to violent crimes. As we have seen in our discussion of the broken windows approach, the general effort at attacking crime problems is to take on the problem of social disorder and use this as a lever against the escalation to violent crime. In the most recent documents released by the Home Office, they suggest that there have been great strides made in dealing with disorder crimes resulting in an overall drop in crime in general. But, the government has also sounded a warning about the persistence of violent crimes, an indication that these types of offenses have resisted the efforts of general disorder policing and pose continued threats to the community.

Where the general principles have worked on a national level, the new directives from the government support a more targeted approach. This involves encouraging local solutions to manage risk and reduce the probability of crime, efforts to reduce fear, and programs that direct attention to the "drivers" of serious crime: drugs, alcohol, and youth. In this instance, then, we see a national strategy of crime prevention that moves from the general to the specific in targeting serious crime, refocusing attention on the risk factors that are more intensely felt in some communities compared to others.

The effectiveness of national strategies to reduce crime has come into question over the years, although the United Kingdom government claims great success in its general programs. In the United States, there has been real doubt expressed about general programs that have been offered as prevention strategies. The best example of this is the mixed experience with Neighborhood Watch programs, which were touted as a solution to the increased threats of crime in urban America.

Neighborhood Watch was started in 1972 and continues to be sponsored by the National Sheriffs' Association (NSA). The aims of the program are to provide a local organizational structure to encourage neighbors to keep watch on their surroundings and to work with local law enforcement in monitoring and controlling crime. As the program is currently constituted, "Neighborhood Watch counts on citizens to organize themselves and work with law enforcement to keep a trained eye and ear on their communities, while demonstrating their presence at all times of the day and night." (The program took off quickly: in just ten years, NSA data showed that 12 percent of the population was involved in a Neighborhood Watch.) Neighborhood Watch is said to work because "it reduces opportunities for crime to occur; it doesn't rely on altering or changing the criminal's behavior or motivation."[1]

Trevor Bennett, Katy Holloway, and David Farrington (2006) suggest that the program has even broader scope, with over a quarter of the United Kingdom population and 40 percent of the population of the United States living in areas covered by Neighborhood Watch programs. The key elements of Neighborhood Watch have been summarized as follows by Bennett and his colleagues. First, there is the most obvious component of the program that has residents of a neighborhood watching out for suspicious activities and reporting them to police. Second, it may also lead to a reduction in opportunities for crime, including creating signals of occupancy such as removing newspapers from homes when people are away on holiday. Third, the process of building a Neighborhood Watch program may lead to increased community interaction and solidarity that, in turn, leads to a greater amount of social resistance to criminal activity. Fourth, these programs may help to provide ongoing information to the police that they can use in curtailing criminal activity using a proactive rather than reactive approach. Finally, an element of the program that encourages marking of property may discourage offenders from stealing as it makes stolen goods more difficult to dispose of (Bennett, Holloway, and Farrington 2006). A key component of the Neighborhood Watch programs includes the development of a local organization run by a block captain. The funding is often, according to Bennett, acquired through local fund-raising and by financial subvention from resources available to the police.

Despite its longevity, widespread adoption, and popularity among law enforcement, there have been critics of this program. In an article published in 1987, Dennis Rosenbaum raised the question of whether or not Neighborhood Watch was a sound fear- and crime-reduction strategy. Its effectiveness was not proven through systematic evaluation, and some negative results suggested that these programs actually raise fear while not reducing crime. In a rigorous review of evaluations performed on Neighborhood Watch programs, Lawrence Sherman and John Eck (Eck 1997) reported no demonstrable effects of these programs on crime prevention.

More recently, Bennett and colleagues (2006) provide the most comprehensive review of all of the studies done to determine the effectiveness of Neighborhood Watch. They present an analysis of findings from eighteen evaluations that met strict criteria of empirical assessment, in particular, a model that allowed for researchers to determine effectiveness based on statistical controls against which treatment effects of the program were compared. In looking at these studies, particularly the results from police as opposed to victim survey data, Bennett and colleagues report a positive effect of the program on crime reduction (although the effects are not overwhelmingly homogeneous as these results were found in only a little over half of the studies). While there is evidence that these programs work, Bennett and his colleagues conclude their study by saying that they are not sure why. They speculate that the program's effectiveness ties to the methods of surveillance, opportunity reduction, and increase in informal social control. However, no study to date has been able to establish these links. Bennett and colleagues have demonstrated that the program is effective in its stated goal, crime reduction, but this is not universally the case across all studies.

Speculation about why it is so hard to prove the effectiveness of these programs rests on weak empirical methods that are applied in evaluation. It is expensive and time consuming to perform a systematic, controlled effects experiment that could consider the impact of this campaign in an area matched against a comparable control. But the campaign Watch initiative has remained popular and widespread, as we have pointed out, despite the mixed evidence of its effectiveness. Now, what if we were to consider this approach in light of our risk model? Consider Neighborhood Watch as a general risk management strategy that really is only effective if set into a larger context of risk assessment and the activities undertaken to reduce the probability of crime. Where this program is integrated into formal law enforcement efforts and programs that target specific threats and initiatives to control disorderly behavior and reduce opportunities, this may be an effective venue for citizens to offer a collective response to crime. Where these other programs do not exist, the effectiveness will be much reduced. As to whether or not these approaches are intrusive or cause greater fear, we acknowledge this as part of our discussion of general threats that we presented above. If these programs become more attuned to the specific concerns within particular areas, their value should increase. We would speculate also that these programs provide a way in which law enforcement agencies can reach community members when police are attempting to develop responses to more specific threats.

This thinking about Neighborhood Watch is consistent with the steps that were taken by police departments to initiate community policing across communities. Community policing is not as strictly programmatic as Neighborhood Watch, which involves specific steps with respect to involvement, recruitment of members, regularized reporting, and so on. Community policing, instead, suggests that police can work with citizens and through teamwork identify and control problems in communities before they get out of control. Both Neighborhood Watch and community policing rest on preemptive assumptions: action taken in advance will reduce the probability of crime, while actions taken immediately following the identification of crime problems reduce the chances of the event recurring.

In order for community policing to work, police agencies designate officers whose role it is to interact with residents in specific locations and to maintain an ongoing dialogue about their environments and the challenges that residents face. This provides the police with a way of identifying issues that have missed their attention before and allows for a more proactive prevention process to be put in place. This approach assumes that policing is more than just responding to crime and making arrests. It involves, as well, dealing with the conditions under which crime emerges and focuses attention on using a broad range of societal resources in eradicating identified problems. Community policing operates as a type of community (bottom-up) risk management approach, by recognizing that some degree of uncertainty in communities comes from a lack of understanding or knowledge about how people in communities interact. Adding residents into the mix—their insights, knowledge, and common sense about how to deal with community problems—reduces the uncertainty stemming from a lack of familiarity and, in a targeted way, helps the police to reduce the community's exposure to crime.

A slightly more sinister view of community policing has been offered by Ericson and Haggerty (1997), who suggest that community policing is really "communication policing," involving the management of information about communities and the people who occupy them through a form of institutional (top-down) risk management. That is, the police gain knowledge of the population in order to control the risks that the population poses rather than the population controlling the risks that they face in their daily lives. In this formulation of community policing, the local police become both keepers of information as well as conduits of information for agencies that make up the larger institutional net of agencies that form the "risk society." Described this way, the community loses control of its environments and is subjugated to the rules of institutional hierarchies. Whether or not this form of control is actually fully integrated between and among agencies of social control, as Ericson and Haggerty have argued—thereby forming a surveillance net that restricts behavior—"risk management" can be a politically loaded term. The factors that are thought to increase the probability of crime are not objectively given: what constitutes risk reflects the organizational values of the political elite rather than those of the community. This suggestion is quite different from what community policing advocates propose in their support of these approaches. The values embedded in the assessment of risk, then, are something we need to look at when we equate risk management with control.

SITUATIONAL CRIME PREVENTION (SPECIFIC/INSTITUTION)

Clarke has made his career looking for ways to prevent crime. In the extensive work that he has done, he has always made a point of connecting a clear understanding of how crime emerges with very specific instructions for what to do about this problem. His work is informed by a point of view that suggests individuals make rational choices about whether or not to commit crimes and they rely on the routine activities of others to make crime opportunities available to them. Clarke makes clear that there are ways in which we can take account of these decisions to commit crimes and stop them through a program of situational crime prevention. Clarke states that this approach departs from conventional criminological approaches in that it looks less at why people commit crime and more directly at the circumstances that lead to crime. This approach introduces

> discrete managerial and environmental change to reduce the opportunity for those crimes to occur. Thus it is focused on the settings for crime, rather than upon those committing criminal acts. It seeks to forestall the occurrence of crime, rather than to detect and sanction offenders. It seeks not to eliminate criminal or delinquent tendencies through improvement of society or its institutions, but merely to make criminal action less attractive to offenders. (Clarke 1997, 2)

This includes what Clarke calls routine precautions, such as locking our doors, as a way of preventing crime from occurring in the first place. When we do this, Clarke suggests that we reduce the risk of crime. In fact, reducing the probability of crime is a central part of the definition of situational crime prevention, where opportunity reduction is directed at specific crimes—it involves the management of the environment in a systematic way—and makes crime more difficult and risky, or "less rewarding and inexcusable by a wide range of offenders" (Clarke 1997, 4).

In this formulation of risk, the offender is considered relative to the event, that is, the choices that are made are reflective of the offender's consideration of the costs involved in committing the crime versus the benefits that might accrue. The costs could include detection and arrest but equally exposure and humiliation. Also, costs can include the amount of effort expended in committing a crime and the resources that might be needed to be successful. The benefits to the offender for successfully completing a crime include financial gain but may also involve revenge, retaliation, and status. In his work, Clarke offers the prescription that if we increase the perceived harm associated with committing a crime (without really understanding how offenders specifically make this calculation) we can prevent this behavior from taking place. Prevention includes the elements of natural surveillance that we have already discussed, but we can add to this specifically targeted surveillance by managers and employees on customers; formal surveillance by security guards; and access control into and out of premises. Each of these strategies is intended to increase the likelihood of detection, coupled with initiatives that make offenders expend more effort to commit crime (e.g., street closures, entry phones, and security plans that include lockdowns).

Situational crime prevention also includes a consideration of risky lifestyles. Although there is no real metric offered about what actually constitutes risky, the general sense is that individuals who live a more public, round-the-clock life that involves proximity to potential offenders are more likely to become victims. A risky lifestyle, essentially, includes behaviors and characteristics that increase the probability of victimization. The risky nature of lifestyles is really a function of the extent to which offenders believe that their targets are easily accessible and may be attacked (or otherwise victimized) with impunity. This goes back to the premise of situational crime prevention that suggests that reducing effort and reducing exposure to punishment will work to increase crime. Many studies have looked at this connection, focusing heavily on results of victimization research. In this work, there is the repeated finding that young people who live public lifestyles are more likely victims of crime (see, for example, Kennedy and Forde 1990; Kennedy and Baron 1993; and Miethe and Meier 1994). Again, the implication is that the public part of their lifestyles makes them easier targets for offenders.

But this research on opportunities for crime has not focused exclusively on public behavior. In some intriguing work by David Finkelhor and Larry Baron (1986), they find a high level of victimization by young people at the hands of offenders who are with them in the home. So, what would appear to be a safe, rather than a high-crime-probability lifestyle—staying at home—is actually transformed into a more potentially hazardous lifestyle given that offenders are less likely to be detected in private quarters (an observation that has been made about domestic violence cases more generally). This problem is compounded, according to Finkelhor and Baron, when the child is living with someone other than a biological parent (a stepfather) and when the mother is away on a regular basis from the home at a job.

In the home, in domestic situations among adults, as we discussed earlier, where much behavior between couples is not publicly scrutinized, there has been increased concern among law enforcement and the public in general that insufficient protection is provided to potential victims who feel inhibited (either because of fear of retaliation or shame) to come forward about violence. We are left, then, with potentially harmful situations that go unresolved for long periods, escalating and deescalating through a cycle of violence. In breaking this cycle, the police have undertaken to take decisive action when they confront injury of any sort (prior to this they had to witness the actual offense; now the injury itself can provide evidence of the abuse taking place). While before they might simply have separated the couple for a cooling-off period, now when police intervene in these cases they are using the force of arrest to provide a decisive step in halting the violence. It is argued that, through this action, the probability of (further) harm to victims is lessened and the abuse may disappear.

Overall, the decisive nature of arrest in reducing violence in family relations is still in question partly because it is not used in all cases (the consensus appears to be that arrest probably takes place in less than half the cases that police encounter). In addition, there is some evidence that arrest may actually have differential effects on different types of offenders. In experiments that were conducted on the effects of different types of police intervention, the goal was "to reduce the risk of repeat violence by the suspect against the same victim in the future" (Sherman 1992, 10). In fact, in some insightful research reported by Sherman (1992) of domestic violence in Minneapolis, the researchers found that individuals who were chronically unemployed would actually increase their violence toward their spouses after being arrested. Sherman speculated that this increase in the probability of offending is derived from the different costs incurred by individuals depending on their circumstances, leading him to suggest that enforcement strategies will have different effects on different groups depending on their social and economic standing.

This presents a challenge to the idea that we simply need to change situations, in this case through arrest, with no regard for the motivation of the offender. In our approach to this, we do not negate situational prevention but rather supplement it, as we are aware that the context presents the bases upon which the assessment of the offender is made. So, it would be possible to increase the costs of crime through prevention strategies to the point that offenders of all backgrounds become aware that the likelihood of detection and punishment is simply not worth the offense. Ramping up to this level, however, is not always possible, although the logic behind mandatory arrests in domestic violence cases was to make the punishment invariant, leaving the outcome highly determined. In those cases, which are many, where the strict application of prevention simply cannot work or is too expensive to apply, consideration needs to be given to the perspective that the offender brings to the situation.

So, the probability of crime, from the situational crime-prevention perspective, can only be reduced if we develop more targeted responses around particular types of crime that make them more hazardous to commit. As Clarke emphasizes, in this approach we worry less about why offenders have a propensity to criminality and more about how they actualize the crimes they commit. Further, Clarke and his colleagues (see, for example, Eck 1993) who have developed this approach are very firm about the idea that, when prevented, crime does not displace to another location—that is, the offender does not simply move to a different place to commit a crime, as it is place specific. Again, for Clarke and colleagues the motivation of the offender and his or her criminality are not really important in the final instance of whether or not the crime occurs.

CRIMINAL CAREERS (SPECIFIC/INDIVIDUAL)

Despite the assertions of situational crime-prevention theorists that the risk of crime lies in the circumstances and not in the offender, related perspectives that focus on the lifestyles of offenders and victims have argued for the importance of considering contexts when judging the likelihood of crime occurrence. As the example from Sherman illustrates, we find there are unexpected negative consequences of intervention strategies, despite the strategy making sense from the point of view of opportunity reduction or increased punishment. Yet, as we discussed earlier, the assumption that all offenders come to situations with the same crime potential and calculate the costs in similar ways is not realistic. While this has most often applied to victims, the idea of offenders' risky lifestyles—lifestyles that increase the probability of involvement in crime—has sparked interest in a number of areas, including research on social control and developmental factors that are said to increase proclivities to offend. Control theories assert that criminals are more likely to lack self-control, and without external pressures to make them conform, they will engage in crime. In other words, low self-control individuals are less likely to be able to regulate their behavior and may actually misjudge the hazards associated with committing crime (Gottfredson and Hirschi 1990).

These same people are harder to deter because they have a different way of calculating their chances of detection and punishment than those with higher levels of self-control. Matt DeLisi (2005) refers to this approach as being part of a group of "propensity theories" that suggest there is some predictability in the ways in which individuals will act and we can, as a consequence, predict their likelihood of offending. The idea that self-control can influence risk calculation is not surprising and is important given the situational crime-prevention assertion that risks of crime are better controlled through management of opportunity rather than managing offenders.

A closer match to situational prevention are developmental theories that include not only the characteristics of offenders that make them more likely to commit crime but also the environmental and community factors that either support or deter them from engaging in criminal behavior. Developmental theorists identify everything from family characteristics, personality and traits, peer influences, and school and neighborhood pressures in the characterization of risk factors for child delinquency and subsequent career criminality (DeLisi 2005, 54). Sampson and John Laub (1990) characterize these social and community factors as important in determining the social capital that individuals accumulate or fail to collect. In the case where social capital is low and informal social control is weak, individual likelihood of participating in criminal behavior increases. Research has shown, though, that where active steps are taken to address the elements of antisocial behavior through the improvement of peer ties, stronger family support, and so on, overall delinquency falls (DeLisi 2005, 120). In a way, this extends the idea of opportunity reduction, but rather than present it as simply a removal of targets, this perspective addresses risk calculation, taking into account that the prospective offender is aware of the moral and social, as well as punishment, costs of delinquency (elements that situational theorists have pointed to as influencing the offender's decision to commit crime). Ultimately, access control and detection provided by surveillance is ramped up to include the important role of informal social sanction.

Yet some individuals continue to commit crime, despite the best efforts to identify antisocial traits and to increase the costs of detection. There are statutes that allow courts to define individuals who are persistent offenders as "chronic" or to assign them a "dangerousness" label. These labels allow more severe and restrictive punishments. Essentially, the courts are encouraged to remove these individuals from opportunities to commit further crimes, assuming that criminal tendencies have not been thwarted by previous punishment. This approach is also taken in dealing with individuals who cannot be held, under the laws, beyond their sentence length but for whom the perceived risk of their reoffending is considered high. In these cases, there have been efforts to control their behaviors through restrictive policies.

The most exemplary of these programs are high-risk offender registries that have been implemented in many states to catalog and make publicly available the names of sex offenders. Offenders, even though they may have already completed their sentences, are deemed a continuing hazard and so are required to register with local police departments. In some jurisdictions, they are precluded from living close to schools or playgrounds. There are even grassroots movements emerging in certain townships to keep ex-convicts from being able to move into these areas. The logic behind these approaches suggests that those who are at risk to offend should be kept away from potential targets, in this case, children. There is an implicit acceptance in this approach that, while not much can be done to make these individuals change their sexual behavior, at least by keeping them away from potential victims, they are less likely to offend (assuming they do not travel to other locations to offend). We discuss these registries at greater length in chapter 4.

We believe that, if we see the discussion of control as relating to risk and attempt to alter the likelihood of crime, this provides a connection to the situational perspective and its consideration of reducing crime probabilities. As Clarke has suggested, weighing the costs and benefits of crime is not only a function of effort but is also impacted through the use of sanctions based on values and morals that are important in society. In a sense, then, we see that, if we distinguish individuals who are more susceptible to making choices that may result in crime from those who are not similarly susceptible, we might have greater success in reducing crime.

With this in mind, there is an argument that would support the surveillance and monitoring of particular offenders or prospective offenders. The principles behind probation and parole include the idea that individuals in these states are at higher risk to reoffend and need (and, in fact, are required) to be monitored. This takes on an even more extreme character as we examine the rationale behind sex offender registers or publication of the names of prostitute's johns. In these cases, not only is the community interested in making these individuals known to others, but also these methods are a means by which people can take steps to remove opportunities for more crimes.

A similar type of program is being suggested to curtail the damage done by individuals with mental issues who may be detected by the system but are often not properly treated for their illnesses. In rare but deadly instances, such as the slayings of students at Virginia Tech and Northern Illinois University, these individuals lose control. Some universities are demanding that students provide information on mental illnesses, but this will be hard to obtain given privacy concerns. And, further, few mentally ill individuals commit serious crimes. At the same time, the conventional approaches offered by situational prevention programs that refer to surveillance or access control are easily overcome in these instances, as the offenders are often members of the community in which they attack and are therefore not likely to trigger suspicion or scrutiny.

SUMMING UP

In our review of the first stage of the risk of crime matrix, we have discussed the different ways in which we identify and prepare for the potential of crime. Some of this response is based on uncertainty where we are not always clear what the specific threat is so we are left to develop general plans to deal with possible incidents. We rely on surveillance, which may not be focused on specific dangers but rather casts a wide net looking for problems. Even then, surveillance strategies, as seen by the evaluation of the effectiveness of CCTV, cannot be claimed to be extremely effective (with some estimates of solution rates—not prevention rates—falling as low as 20 percent). But surveillance has grown to be extremely popular among both the public and law enforcement and is now widespread, raising questions beyond its effectiveness, to the extent to which trolling for threats in uncertainty compromises our privacy and freedom from interference in pursuing legal day-to-day activities.

Beyond surveillance, a more focused approach is offered by "quality of life" approaches that address the risk of exposure to social disorder, as opposed to the treatment of criminality per se. The avowed strategy in this perspective is to deal with minor problems before they lead to larger ones. While the perspective does not specifically address the relationship between minor and major crimes (i.e., whether there are certain predictable outcomes that result from addressing quality of life crimes), the advocates of this approach provide a rationale that is consistent with the view that reducing exposure to social and physical disorder will reduce actual crime. It is important for this perspective that social disorganization arising in communities that is left unchecked can lead to behavior that is criminal. And this disorganization is not just based on physical decline. It also derives from difficulties faced by communities in combating crime based on social disorder.

A key element in the broken windows perspective is the extent to which social decay and minor incivilities raise the fear levels of community members, making them less likely to resist the conditions that encourage crime. In exploring fear we see that it ties directly to perceptions of the risk of crime, as the heuristics offered by prospect theory make clear. This approach suggests that individuals will gauge their vulnerability based on their assessment of the environment, what others tell them, and their own and others' experiences. Perceived vulnerability will govern their actions and influence the overall extent to which they will engage in supporting efforts, through informal social control, to reduce crime.

This form of prevention takes into account how the situations that people find themselves in can impact their behavior, particularly in discouraging offending. Through situational approaches, attention is paid to opportunity reduction and target hardening. Yet, it is clear that individuals come to these situations with different assessments of the likelihood of getting caught or being punished. As a result, we have explored the idea that risk models of situational approaches need to consider the importance of lifestyles, bringing into this discussion some of the findings of criminologists who have looked at criminal careers and developmental approaches to crime. While these approaches have really not been considered in light of the powerful effects of situational approaches to crime prevention, in the context of risk assessment, it would be possible to search for heuristics used by offenders to guide their offending behavior in order to make judgments about the success of their actions (based on avoiding detection and arrest, primarily) in a way that parallels our discussion of heuristics used by victims in determining their security.

In the next chapter, at the second stage of crime risk, we begin to look at the contexts and scripts of behavior patterns that individuals follow in the actual crime incident.

NOTE

1. National Crime Prevention Council, "Neighborhood Watch: Tools and Resources to Help You Start or Maintain a Neighborhood Watch Program," at www.ncpc.org/topics/home-and-neighborhood-safety/neighborhood-watch (accessed June 2009).

3

Crime Transactions

Crime transactions can be viewed from a number of perspectives. They are individual events, the outcome of the relationship between the victim and offender. Crimes are situations, abetted by social disorder or poor social control. Or, crimes can be viewed as a consequence of broad, sweeping social factors that influence housing markets, neighborhood revival, and policing strategies. The transaction is the core of the crime risk matrix. Without the transaction, the risk is only putative. With the transaction, we have evidence that, in the actualization of the incident, the offender "assumed risk"; whether rationally or not, the offender determined that the benefits outweighed the negative and committed the crime. This act precipitates numerous consequences and can cause a wide range of responses, from police action to legal responses to fear. Understanding transactions from the point of view of risk helps us make sense of how we can manage situations and their consequences to reduce the likelihood of future incidents. We can manage outcomes from an individual perspective or from a more global policy viewpoint. We will begin with the latter with a look at crime waves.

CRIME WAVES (GENERAL/STATE)

When the term "super-predator" made its way into the popular lexicon in the early 1990s, the crime problem appeared to be out of control. There were stories about gangs of young men swarming innocent victims in parks and on city streets, beating them mercilessly, stealing their jewelry and money, and leaving them for dead. The assailants appeared remorseless and impossible to deter. They swaggered in front of their victims and were, it was said, triggered into violence by inadvertent slights that came from something as innocuous as a stare. The view of the mayhem perpetrated by the super-predator was fueled by interviews with young offenders caught up in what were seen as senseless crimes of violence, including random attacks on the elderly. When they discussed the motivation for their actions, these young men (and they were primarily young men) would say they had no special reason for the violence; they just felt like it, underlining further the sense-lessness of their actions.

Riding the popular view of youth out of control, John DiUlio, a political scientist, weighed in with a prediction that not only were these super-predators a threat to our society but also they would start appearing in ever larger numbers (he was joined in this prediction by others, most notably James Fox [1996], an expert on homicide, who foretold a large run-up on murders in the following decades as a result of the growth in numbers of this highly aggressive and violent group). DiUlio (1995) argued that we would have a wave of violence that would be undeterred through conventional means. He called for an attack on juvenile crime and encouraged stricter policing and tougher sentences against youth to keep them from causing the damage that would inevitably ensue from their lack of control. The public reacted to these calls, demanding that politicians act. Governments passed bills to punish these individuals more severely, guaranteeing longer stays in prison. The outcry met some resistance by researchers who argued that this phenomenon of super-predator was not clearly evidenced in the overall patterns of juvenile crime (Zimring 1998), but the media-inspired moral panic ensued nonetheless (Pizarro, Chermak, and Gruenewald 2007).

Interestingly enough, just as this call for more punitiveness developed, a steady drop in crime had begun. More importantly, the prediction concerning the growth in the super-predator population simply did not come true. While the numbers of youth involved in crime stayed high, their involvement in violent crime at an extraordinary rate suggested by the super-predator proph-ecy did not appear. After a number of years, DiUlio actually withdrew his prediction in face of the evidence that he had been wrong. But it has taken many years to begin to redress some of the consequences of his prediction, including harsh drug sentencing laws that were drawn up at least in part as a result of his dire prophecy. If we look carefully at this example, we see in it the elements of a general unease that comes from interpreting individual events, such as a gang attack, as a general phenomenon. Put in risk terms, the population develops strong concerns about the apparent surge in certain types of crime and pressures the state to respond to reduce the likelihood of future events, even if the response does not necessarily directly impact the problem.

Vince Sacco has spent many years thinking about and writing about the rise and fall of crime and the social reactions to these changes. In his book *When Crime Waves* (2005), he suggests that we consider the drama around crime surges less as "moral panics" and more as "crime waves" to denote less an unreasonable response and, instead, a characterization of reactions that coincide with some change in the public views of their susceptibility to crime hazards. With this change in terms, Sacco brings us more closely in our understanding of the collective reactions to crime to a risk-based model, one that is based more closely on threats and hazards rather than on the emotional and irrational responses that a moral panic connotes.

According to Sacco, crime waves constitute four elements. First, the term is used to describe more serious rather than less serious crime. Second, this term is used to describe common crimes, such as theft and robbery, rather than crimes committed by corporations or businesses. Third, this term tends to be used to describe crimes that occur in nonintimate situations more often than between people known to one another. Crime waves can include descriptions of trends involving victims (e.g., missing children), offenders (e.g., super-predators), criminal events (e.g., home invasion), or places (e.g., school violence; Sacco 2005, 15). Again, the implication here is not that these crimes do not occur but rather that they take on characteristics of threat that are socially constructed to be more prevalent than they actually are in real numbers.

This social construction is particularly interesting to us in our discussion of risk. When we referred earlier to how people calculate the occurrence of certain types of dangers (based on the previously mentioned Slovic research), we reported the finding that they are often not very accurate in their assessments, overstating some dangers and understating others. Crime waves are a collective phenomenon formed by these miscalculations: large numbers of people miscalculate the threat that is posed by particular events. Even more interesting is that, in cases of concerns about certain types of threats, the perceived probability of their likelihood rises or falls over time. The risk assessment is not only disconnected from the actual numbers of crimes that might (or have) occur(ed), or offenders involved in certain types of crimes, but there is also a change in the ways in which the public views the problem over time (even if the actual occurrences of the crimes do not change over this time period). This wave effect is partly a function of increased information about threats that may change people's judgments of risk, but it is also based on the extent to which people believe that the threat is something that necessarily affects them. This is a decision that might be heavily influenced by discussions with others, by listening to media sources, or by the debates they hear involving experts or policy makers. The wave may also dissipate, though, when other concerns emerge as more dramatic or threatening (referred to as "valence value" by Malcolm Spector and John Kitsuse [1973]). Valence value may not only change the relative importance of concerns but also influence our calculation of risk related to these concerns.

The emphasis on juvenile crime, with the high valence value provided by the attachment of an emotion-laden term such as super-predator, provides an illustration of a social issue that takes on importance beyond the evidence. Other examples include the child kidnapping scares that developed based on a few highly publicized cases. As Joel Best (1990) has clearly demonstrated, the actual risk of child abduction was much less (based on actual statistics) than was stated in media accounts of this crime. Similarly, we witness the intense interest in carjacking (a rare but highly terrifying crime for the victims) and home invasions (again a crime that evokes high levels of fear, played on by widespread advertising by home protection companies, but one that actually occurs rarely). Accompanying rising concerns about these crimes, there is often a widespread call for action, frequently resulting in dramatic public statements by politicians on the need to crack down on these crimes, often accompanying a set of policy initiatives that range from new programs to new enforcement strategies. This is not to say that crime increases need to be ignored but rather that there is, at times, a disjuncture between what is perceived as threatening and the likelihood of harm that these threats pose to public safety.

MANAGING THREAT INFORMATION (GENERAL/INSTITUTION)

When we move closer in our model to actual incidents, we see that institutions develop ways to anticipate threats. The more general approaches use surveillance and prevention strategies, as we talked about in the previous chapter. Threats are brought to the attention of authorities through the development of intelligence strategies that rely on tips, local information, and police investigation to generate a more detailed picture of why certain types of crimes are occurring. Intelligence, operating at this level, originates from careful study of why and how problems are occurring, for example, the development of drug markets or the increase in auto thefts. This information then moves its way into the intelligence stream through attribution of responsibilities and tapping sources that can confirm certain information. Intelligence is often law enforcement sensitive and carefully guarded to protect informants and police tactics. It is a vital aspect of investigations and is valuable in not only anticipating new crimes but also breaking up activities that may be contributing to an ongoing series of crimes.

This information is considered in the context of the "intelligence cycle," which is pictured below (figure 3.1).

This model is based on an assumption that the agency collecting the information has a strategic plan that lays out the general principles of detection and response that forms the bases for its actions. At the top of the cycle the agency sets out its plans and direction. It then moves to collect information about the concerns that it has identified (for example, problems with gangs, drug enforcement, ties of organized crime groups to terrorists, and so on). From here, there is an analysis phase where data are reviewed and trends and patterns identified. This analysis is then disseminated to members of the agency who are responsible for developing action plans. The final stage involves the evaluation of the quality of the intelligence and its effectiveness in support of the goals of the organization. This intelligence-gathering process then leads to subsequent cycles of problem identification, data collection, and so on.

The intelligence model has been adopted by law enforcement, forming what is referred to as "intelligence-led policing." Jerry Ratcliffe (2003) explains this as "the application of criminal intelligence analysis as an objective decision-making tool in order to facilitate crime reduction and prevention through effective policing strategies and external partnership projects drawn from an evidential base" (3). Ratcliffe emphasizes that three components to this form of policing—the interpretation of intelligence, the influence this has

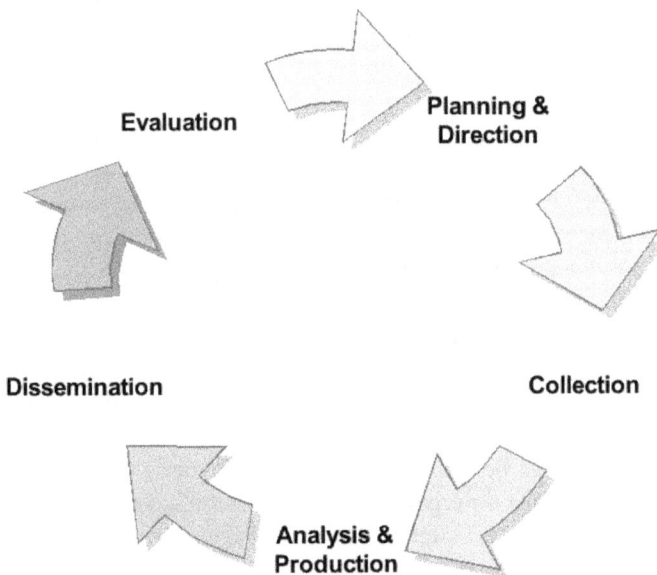

Figure 3.1. The Intelligence Cycle (adapted from Fuentes, 2006).

on decision makers, and the ultimate impact this has on the criminal environment—all contribute to crime prevention. Intelligence is a constant process of data collection, analysis, distribution, and assessment, and can be created by specialized groups, crime analysts, or the police members themselves. Intelligence-led policing is proactive rather than reactive and continuously changes as each of the three elements (intelligence, decision makers, and criminal environment) change.

Part of the impetus for this movement toward intelligence-led policing has been the changing demands that have been put on police as a result of terrorism attacks. Police researchers have suggested that the secret to counterterrorism efforts in the United States and elsewhere is the action of local police in addressing common crimes that lead to terrorist acts. In support of this view, it has been observed that 650,000 local police officers are more effective in deterring terrorism than a few thousand federal agents. The idea is that, because local police are "closer to the action" (street), they are in a better position to detect anomalous behaviors or clues to behavior—clues that may signal terrorism plans underway or, in a better case scenario, terrorism plans in the early planning stages. Thwarting plans in progress is a form of risk management: reducing the likelihood of grand-scale attacks. Further, the information that local authorities collect form a critical ingredient in piecing together threats to national security.

Police agencies have been increasingly called upon to develop plans for emergencies that might result from attacks, to upgrade their equipment (particularly communication technology), and to participate, through training and information sharing, in multiagency counterterrorism task forces. The by-product of this sudden rush to preparedness has been an increased importance placed on data management to detect threats. Intelligence-led policing has provided the framework for this form of strategic change. Also, it has been facilitated by modern information management technology that had been introduced over the last few years. In its most raw form, there has been discussion of what is referred to as the crime/terror nexus, which refers to the fact that all terrorism involves some sort of criminal action.

The police are instrumental in attacking crime that connects to terrorism and have a role to play in this nexus. This would involve a number of things including providing information about suspects, identifying suspicious behavior that might be connected to preterrorist activity, or cracking down on crimes that might be a prelude to terror. It is in the latter category that some controversy has emerged about the usefulness of this type of police work. For example, the Federal Bureau of Investigation (FBI) has designated as a precursor crime to terrorism the manufacture and acquisition of fake identification. On the surface, this type of supposition appears to make sense, particularly as terrorists who are not legally in the country need ID to go through access points at airports, open bank accounts, drive cars, and so on. Where there might be a ring of counterfeiters operating in an area, they may be offering their services to terrorists. In assessing the crime data in an area, then, law enforcement has been alerted to watch for these types of bogus IDs. Similarly, law enforcement has been alerted to the activity of gangs that might support terrorists, through bank robberies to get money or through the peddling of arms. The thinking is that certain types of crimes are problematic in and of themselves, but they may also foreshadow other types of crimes or events such as terrorism that are not as obvious from previous behavior.

This type of reasoning suggests the need for greater vigilance and more detailed analysis of crime trends and patterns. However, we need to approach this nexus with some caution. While it may be the case that terrorist crimes have counterfeiting as their precursor, there is likely a preponderance of counterfeiting that has nothing to do with terrorism. It is not uncommon for fake IDs to appear on college campuses to facilitate underage drinking,[1] which are clearly not to help gain access to chemical plants for illicit purposes, such as blowing them up. So, the efforts that are needed to sort the precursors from the false predictors are enormous, and the indicators truly lack precision on their own. However, through a carefully constructed intelligence plan that combines the identification of these types of false predictors with others that presage violent outbursts, we can make more sense of the nexus. The problem really lies in that we are looking at one type of information (crime data), often of high frequency, to help us make sense of another, low-frequency type of activity (terrorism). The degree to which one source of data at one level can be used to interpret another source at another level is not clear. We really don't understand the intricate ways in which this nexus combines these two types of events.

One way that has been suggested to resolve this problem is that we adopt better analytical schemes in our use of crime data. In addressing this information flow, much has been made of the integration of key data sources and the manipulation and assessment of this information as intelligence. Matched up with the intelligence that is generated at the federal level, it is argued, a much more sophisticated counterintelligence program should emerge. Given this view, it seems fair that we begin an assessment of the challenges that this perspective presents and the prospects that it offers in advancing our thinking about the interplay between local and state authorities. The recent growth in the United States of state-level "data fusion centers" designed to collect and analyze information is a recent response to the Justice Information Sharing mandate toward integrating data sources from all levels of agencies.

DATA FUSION CENTERS AND SECURITY NETWORKS

From the published guidelines describing their role,

> The ultimate goal of a fusion center is to provide a mechanism where law enforcement, public safety, and private partners can come together with a common purpose and improve the ability to safeguard our homeland and prevent criminal activity. A police officer, fireman, or building inspector should not have to search for bits of information. They should know to call one particular place—the jurisdiction's fusion center.[2]

But getting the information into fusion centers in a form that is standardized, and making it easily available to users has posed immense challenges. In particular, the sheer size of the data flow is so great that it becomes a huge task to compile all the information. Then, there is the need to have a clear plan for how these data should be analyzed. As they stand, they may simply be treated as having equal weight (the information from one source, for example, may be considered as useful as that from another source). It is the task of these organizations to begin to make sense of the dangers that these data direct us to and to provide analysis that addresses them. This has meant, inevitably, that the fusion centers have been most preoccupied with crime analysis as crime threats are constant and immediate. Planning for low-incidence terrorist events is more difficult. The data that can be used in these cases relate more to generalized threats, as opposed to the tracking we can do of actual crime incidents. It is inevitable that these fusion centers will spend more time looking at crime than terrorism, which makes sense given the concern over mitigating ongoing threats. There is concern, however, that the fusion centers are not meeting their goals if they become crime data centers. Their support and mission was clearly specified as targeting terrorism. The impetus for building these centers came from national security concerns. And yet, can we justify maintaining large and expensive data-management centers that target only terror, however important this is in terms of overall consequence for the society?

Going beyond the strictly utilitarian answer that suggests workload should dictate where resources are spent, we can look at a more general answer connecting to the overall concerns that appear in a newly insecure society still reeling from the effects of a terrorist attack. This tension is expressed in an article about Providence, Rhode Island, where the city police have been trying to come to grips with the incongruity of the tasks that they face (Johnson 2008). They continue to get federal money to fight terrorism while the grants for crime fighting continue to drop. This has left the chief and others frustrated about how to set priorities, particularly as, in the years since the

World Trade Center attacks, there has not been one substantiated terror attack in Providence. Yet, at the same time there has been a rapid increase in inner-city violence particularly focused on gangs (as we discussed previously). The police have little choice in terms of where they focus their efforts, as they need to deal with the problem of violence and they benefit from the shared information they receive from the interagency support that has developed since 9/11. At the same time, the emphasis of the federal agencies does not comport with those of local police. It is difficult with this scenario to really take too seriously the advantage of having 650,000 officers looking for terrorists when they rarely, if ever, catch one.

Changing this focus will be difficult in the short run. Targeting resources based on uncertain threats can be problematic and lead to frustration for those whose task is to address more immediate concerns. This tension offers interesting insight into the problems that come in defining threats. It illustrates the many difficulties that get in the way of having states work together to achieve common goals. As we have just noted, if individuals do not define past events in the same way, it seems even less likely to expect that states will define situations similarly. Yet, as Aristotle observed a long time ago, "A common danger unites even the bitterest enemies"—a post-9/11 world appears to provide a number of common dangers. This is a central component of states working together: the threat must be specific and direct in order to bring together otherwise separate entities. Abstract threats leave too much room for interpretation, and in the face of abstract threats states will determine that their resources are better placed elsewhere.

Policing and security networks consist of three entities: state, market, and communitarian. Within each of these entities there are further divisions—the state policing system is typically divided into civilian and military agencies; market security entities may consist of private and corporate agencies; and communitarian security may involve voluntary community and victims' groups (Gill 2006, 29). Peter Gill suggests that, although these entities overlap to varying degrees, they also have varying levels of "depth" (primarily consisting of transnational, national, and local/regional issues) and are hierarchically connected to each other. In the pursuit of reducing the risk of further harm (by addressing particular problems or people), what is of interest is the manner in which these levels and entities come together (or fail to come together); the connections that form particular security networks; the social relations that evolve; and the distinctions that may be made between intelligence (which tends to be forward looking) and evidence (which tends to be backward looking). Security networks move beyond national borders and reveal the ways in which the domestic policing of a particular nation may be influenced by the external relationships a specific nation has with others.

As we pointed out above, security networks are based upon the "gathering and storing of information" (Gill 2006, 27), or intelligence, and the information that is up for trade. Increasingly, information is traded between public agencies, between public and private agencies, as well as between nations. As Gill points out, the idea behind security networks is to "'join the dots' between items of information already in the system." Efforts to "join the dots," however, are often hampered by a general reluctance by agencies to divulge information without a certain payback, with high premiums placed on "sensitive information" (Gill 2006, 37). This reluctance has been addressed to a certain degree by establishing "brokerages"—fusion centers or task forces—to navigate the collection of data to deal with particular issues. Gill explains that representatives from various agencies who have access to their own databases are brought together to combine resources "of otherwise separate agencies on a targeted problem or person by overcoming the incompatibility of different databases or privacy restrictions on the sharing of information" (37). Importantly, the "dots" that are joined are specific information about specific threats.

How are security networks managed? The short answer is "not easily." Gill clarifies, first, that diversity within and between agencies reduces the ability to manage networks effectively, as greater diversity also suggests differential constraints on participation in a security network. Second, security networks also tend to be closed systems, built on the trade of information that is not accessible to all who ask for it (Gill 2006, 39). While closed systems may self-regulate, the secrecy of their operations poses some difficulties. A third issue is that of conflict and convergence of interests (39). Not all parties to a security network prioritize various dangers in similar ways. A fourth factor is the social context in which fusion centers are working (40). Problems may be differentially profiled in certain areas over others, or the media, for example, may increase public pressure to "do something" about a particular issue. Fifth, Gill notes that the history and success of previous dealings between agencies determines the likelihood of sharing information. Trust is clearly paramount, and bringing agencies "on side" that have histories of problematic relations is difficult if not impossible—common enemy or not. Finally, as we have noted elsewhere (Van Brunschot and Kennedy 2008), resources come in to play with participation in security networks possibly involving costs that are differentially onerous depending upon the participating agency.

In outlining some of the issues associated with managing security networks, we also get a sense of the difficulties associated with the oversight of these networks that draw upon the participation of a number of agencies at a variety of levels and across countries. As Gill points out, hierarchical structures are not necessarily efficient structures, but they have the advantage of demarcating clear lines of accountability. In contrast, security networks do not have accountability structures "built in." While networks attempt to manage and deal with risk by reducing the probability of negative events, the idea of all being "in this together" does not necessarily bypass or address management and accountability issues. Accountability relates also to the concept of due process and protecting the rights of individuals identified as security threats.

It is not yet clear how these data-integration programs will work and how intelligence-led policing will apply in the U.S. police environment. The question about whether fusion centers focus primarily on crime analysis becomes a much more complicated issue around networks, sharing, accommodation, and accountability. This has everything to do with changing the focus from reactive strategies to more proactive, risk-based intelligence approaches.

Challenges abound in making this shift, including disagreements over standardization, jurisdiction, access limitations, training, and cooperation across agencies. The United Kingdom is particularly interesting in this regard as they have made some important first steps in implementing an intelligence-led policing program that has at its core a National Intelligence Model that purports to standardize police reporting, analysis, and intelligence-based actions. Tim John and Mike Maguire (2004) explain the challenges faced by this new intelligence model. In particular, they raise questions concerning the roles that key leadership will play in making this form of intelligence-based model work. The successes that come in innovation are due to the commitment and involvement of those who administer the policy. Police leadership may begin to utilize this approach to reach more effective outcomes if they are convinced of its ability to address crime potential. In fact, as John and Maguire assert, the National Intelligence Model is constructed to move police commanders' awareness from response to particular crimes to a more strategic, risk-based approach in identifying areas of concern and developing resource-allocation strategies. The intelligence drawn from police analysts, police officers on the beat, and information gathered from targeted surveillance combines to inform risk assessments that direct future police action (we will present a model of how risk assessment can work in police agencies in chapter 5). John and Maguire suggest that this assessment include much more than reports on crime; it should also involve the scrutiny and assessment of business operations, demographic change, crime networks, and so on (John and Maguire 2004).

This shift in police focus, from a narrowly defined crime detection and response strategy to a much more broadly based assessment of exposure to crime threats, encourages a multiagency plan to manage both social disorder and insecurity. Yet as Maguire (2000) points out, this shift from passive surveillance to active risk management has its dangers, as the concerns about privacy and use of invasive practices are harder to control with such a wide scope of police action. This danger is further enhanced as intelligence, unlike general surveillance, is specifically targeted toward particular individuals and groups. This type of risk management is an aggressive form of information collection and decision-making processes requiring huge police resources. The urge to press hard on targeted offenders may result in what Maguire has referred to as a "proportionality" problem, where huge pressure is exerted to stop the actions of individuals involved in minor crimes (326).

More to the point, while there has been some enthusiastic response to this form of coordinated, intelligence-based policing, there is still work to do to establish its actual effectiveness. Does targeting offenders or groups of offenders result in a reduction of crime in contrast to applying standard police patrol and control strategies? Do these targeted approaches actually reduce the probability of crime (or terrorism)? Certainly, while there are those who would say that the effectiveness of intelligence-based programs, such as Operation Ceasefire, which we turn to next, provides ample evidence of the value of this approach in reducing drug-related violence, the more general application of these approaches has not been fully assessed.

OPERATION CEASEFIRE

The initial Operation Ceasefire program was put in place in Boston. It began as the Boston Gun Project in 1995 under the direction of David Kennedy, Anthony Braga, and Anne Piehl from the John F. Kennedy School of Government at Harvard. The strategy behind this initiative was an attack on illegal gun trafficking and the implementation of a strong deterrent to gang violence. According to Kennedy et al. (2001), the basic steps of the program involved the following:

- Assembling an interagency working group of largely line-level criminal justice and other practitioners.
- Applying quantitative and qualitative research techniques to assess the nature of and dynamics driving youth violence in Boston.
- Developing an intervention designed to have a substantial near-term impact on youth homicide.
- Implementing and adapting the intervention.
- Evaluating the intervention's impact. (1)

This highly targeted approach to gun violence combined a direct attack on gun distributors, as well as gang members, using "levers" against them to deter them from future crime. But, importantly, this approach also included a community-based initiative that recruited social services, parole and probation agencies, and community members to offer gang members alternatives to street crime through the services provided by these agencies. In addition to this targeted effort, Operation Ceasefire was directly involved in the assessment of its program's success, measured in terms of reduced violence but also in terms of a reduction in drug trafficking in the targeted areas. The Operation Ceasefire program has been replicated with some success in other areas (Tita, Riley, and Greenwood 1994), and violence-reduction programs have also been implemented in other cities (Braga, McDevitt, and Pierce 2006; McGarrell et al. 2006; U.S. Department of Justice 2006).

From a risk-based point of view, these approaches are hazard based, and targeting is very specifically directed against repeat, high-violence individuals in high-crime areas. The idea is that, by targeting these individuals, their likelihood of continuing to commit crime is much reduced. Further, the violence and disorder their activities engender will also be reduced. The risk is also mitigated, to a degree, with alternative programs that individuals can take advantage of, if they choose, but if they choose not to change their violent ways they are pressured directly by law enforcement action (McGarrell et al. 2006). The direct use of coordinated information across agencies and the follow-up evaluation of program effectiveness help keep these programs accountable and the targeting of problems much more precise than standard response-based policing.

There have been challenges to this form of risk-based policing, suggesting that it is insensitive to the views of community members and does not properly address their concerns arising from fear and insecurity. As the argument goes, the risk-based approach appears to drive an aggressive, centrist approach to police response that is insensitive to local concerns or to the need for a more consumer-oriented approach on the part of police. This approach specifically targets the individuals and groups most often identified as problematic by formal agents of social control. In a sense, this criticism, which in the United Kingdom has revolved around the movement toward the creation of reassurance and community-based policing, appears to reject the importance of threats and probable harms to the ways in which the public and the police approach crime. In reaction to an intelligence-based approach, the criticism is that risk has been commodified by police agencies into units of control that have some objective, immutable character to them (measured in terms of quantity of police action, resource targeting, and so on). But this view does not align with the ways in which we have referred to risk in this book, where it evolves from interpretations that different actors bring to social interactions and their perceptions of personal security.

Our understanding encourages information gathering and proactive-response agency planning but does not negate the idea that risk interpretations may vary by group or location. This point is underlined in an excellent review by Maguire and John of the tension that has developed in the United Kingdom between new initiatives in policing (particularly to accommodate local concerns) and the introduction of the National Intelligence Model. The reversion to local, more traditional policing strategies might appear to support the idea that these are set in opposition to intelligence-led policing:

> However, while this may be the case if "intelligence led policing" is understood in the relatively narrow sense of a set of processes kept "within the police" and based mainly on analysis of police information about specific criminals and criminal groups, there is a broader interpretation of the meaning of intelligence led policing that is less threatened by the new developments mentioned. This interpretation is reflected in the National Intelligence Model, which, far from being simply a vehicle for the promotion of proactive methods of investigation (such as the use of surveillance and informants and the preparation of target operations against prolific offenders), offers a framework of business processes for the management of policing priorities of all kinds. If implemented as intended, it incorporates into its analytical processes the views of, and evidence and information from, both partner agencies and members of local communities, takes account of community problems as well as crime, and sets guidelines and parameters for reactive as well as proactive investigations. In other words, despite the vagaries of shifts in public and media concerns, and the increasingly populist and emotive nature of crime related debates, the structured use of analysis within the Model potentially takes full account of these factors, yet at the same time retains an essentially evidence based process of decision making and prioritization, as well as a "forward looking" focus on predicted crime trends or other threats to community safety. (Maguire and John 2006, 83)

However we approach threats, if we want to become more proactive in our plans and make more efficient use of our resources, it is important that we adapt an information-based approach in defining risks and opportunities. Beyond this, as we have argued, there should be accountability. We will talk about this in later chapters, but for now it is important to note that information is not just collected to identify whom to target or where we need to put resources. Information is also collected to provide us with the opportunity to evaluate how well our plans have worked and whether or not we need to adjust or change our interventions to make them more effective. The importance of risk-based information and intelligence is that it can be used to anticipate both potential opportunities and potential harm, at the same time enabling the deciphering of past factors that have been more highly correlated with harmful or beneficial outcomes.

There is a strong impetus provided within the field of criminology to underline the importance of empirically based assessment of programs. Through the efforts of the Campbell Collaboration,[3] more rigorous studies of crime causation are being done. We have talked about results from a couple of these in previous pages (Welsh and Farrington 2001; Lum, Kennedy, and Sherley 2006). Information structured for more rigorous scientific testing should be a goal that we set in our approaches to integrating risk management strategies into crime control and prevention.

MULTIPLE VICTIMIZATION (GENERAL/INDIVIDUAL)

Crime victimization surveys, unlike official statistics that rely on reports of police arrests, focus instead on the reports of victims. Over the last twenty years, victimization surveys show that the levels of reported victimization have, overall, dropped in half. Although it is true that victimization numbers are higher than official statistics, in the last few years there has been a convergence in the reported levels of victimization and the crimes known to the police (although, nationwide in the United States, the reported victimization levels of serious violent crime in the mid-2000s are still double the arrests made by police).[4]

Analysts who have looked at this pattern have alerted us to the fact that the discrepancy between the levels of reporting in official statistics and the differing pattern in victim statistics suggests there are two different systems at work in generating these crime numbers. As we pointed out in the previous section, official statistics are reflective of intervention strategies adopted by police and other agencies to control and reduce the probability of crime. The victim statistics may include police actions, but add to this the accounting of crime incidence by victims who interpret these behaviors as criminal but who have not sought criminal sanction against the offender. These victimization numbers account for the hazards that individuals face in different circumstances and under different conditions. They also take into account the idea that crime acts only exist within a larger context.

We have two coexistent crime accounting systems, then, not just one. The first deals with the extent to which crime poses a threat to us as documented by the activity of the police in the management of the danger that results. The other takes note of the interpretations of victims in defining their experience with crime and suggests a probability of crime that individuals in similar circumstances may encounter. While crime rates document a formally structured account of crime hazards and opportunities, victimization rates document a process whereby individuals have encountered criminal hazards and how they have dealt with them, including, but not necessarily, reporting them to the police. The two rates of crime cannot easily be compared to one another. This is not surprising when we think of the former as an indicator of hazard and the latter as indices of risk: crime rates are based on the formal determination of a crime hazard, while victimization rates reflect individuals' perceptions of the hazards and harms experienced—regardless of how they are reported. While crime rates provide an annotated measure of the structure of how police, criminals, and victims have come together to define an event as criminal—they do not necessarily provide any indication as to what the future holds. Similarly, victim surveys do not indicate future probabilities; they simply indicate how it is that individuals have defined their previous involvements—as (crime) losses. Yet, they also provide a more accurate description of how individuals perceive the threats and hazards in their environments.

The discussion of data from victimization surveys in contrast to the numbers generated by the police has focused on the extent to which the gap between these numbers is influenced by the victim's willingness to report crime experiences. A number of reasons have been given for this reluctance, including fear of the police, uncertainty about the crime, desire to protect the offender, and fear of the offender (Kennedy and Sacco 1998). The reasons given for not reporting to the police constitute a basis upon which we can assess victim endangerment as separate from how this is defined by the police. As we pointed out, however, this gap has not stayed constant over time. Rather, the gap has been closing—interestingly enough, this appears to occur as a result of victimization rates decreasing while crime rates drop, but less quickly. This might be interpreted as meaning that, while interpretations of threats have diminished, realized hazard, in the form of recorded crime, has also dropped independently. Yet, is this likely to be the case? It may be: if people are working to protect themselves more effectively, thereby reducing their exposure to danger, this may translate into more dramatic drops in victim rates. Meanwhile, the police may be more efficient in managing hazards and dealing with crime occurrence (possibly in ways other than formally charging offenders).

Following this logic, at a certain point, the management of risk should translate into a lagged decline in official crime rates, which, we could argue, may be the case. But equally, it could be the case that the incidents drop and the perception of hazards change, as measured in the victimization surveys. The connections between official crime and victimization are clearly artifacts of a measurement and reporting process, but the distinction between hazard and risk is more than reporting. It suggests a distinction between how the police manage crime through official accounts and arrests and what victims experience (both reporting and not reporting crime; Akins et al. 2003).

What seems to be a confusing picture derives from our inability to separate what crime rates and victim rates represent. Particularly problematic in our interpretation is the constant focus on official crime rates as a monitor of crime experience, often interpreted as risk. For example, real estate agents tend to use official crime rates as an index of how "safe" particular neighborhoods may be. We know, however, that the probability of personal harm (which is what the public is concerned with) is better deduced from victimization rates rather than crime rates. Further, the confusion over what has led to crime rate drops may be due to the differences in the types of data that are used to identify the likelihood of crime events.

Important factors influencing this debate are the extent to which individuals are exposed to crime and their perceptions of the degree to which they are likely to become victims. Steven Balkin (1979) suggests that we need to pay careful attention to the degree to which differential exposure to crime problems can influence the risks that individuals take as influenced by their fear. Further, Ronnie Janoff-Bulman and Irene Frieze (1983) suggest that psychological states that encourage individuals to develop an "illusion of invulnerability" can be maladaptive if these keep people from engaging in effective preventive behaviors or cause them to be slow to recognize that a crime is taking place. This attentiveness to danger can vary by situation or by individual, suggesting that the probability of victimization can be influenced by not only actual hazard but also perceptions. The concern about vulnerability may be based on behavioral self-blame that forces individuals to reconsider their personal security and drives them to reassess the steps they take to protect themselves. This self-protection includes using strategies that preclude theft and avoiding areas that are considered unsafe. It may also lead to more aggressive responses where individuals use retaliation to change the odds of victimization (a problem that occurs, for example, in the reactions among the street youth that Stephen Baron, David Forde, and Leslie Kennedy [2007] have studied).

A surprising finding that comes from the study of victimization, however, raises some questions about whether or not people's vulnerability changes that much in the aftermath of victimization. Based on the 1992 British Crime Survey (BCS), reported research findings suggest that half of those who were victimized were repeat victims (the same result has shown up in all subsequent victimization surveys). Further, this group suffered 81 percent of all reported crimes (Walklate 1997). Also from this study, evidence shows that the 4 percent who experienced four or more crimes a year accounted for 44 percent of all crime. If we were to suspect that these individuals had distinctive characteristics that made them more vulnerable, however, Denise Osborn et al. (1996) quickly disabuse us of this conclusion. They find no evidence that multiply victimized households were different from those victimized only once. What the research indicates is that those who reported themselves as being at low initial risk of victimization are also least likely to experience multiple victimization. The researchers believe this means that the factors putting people in danger in the first place are what make them victims in subsequent events. But, these factors obviously go beyond the demographic characteristics of the victims and include contextual factors that increase vulnerability, a point supported by Balkin's (1979) research on differential exposure. It does not stop there. The findings from the BCS pointing to the concentration of victimization effects led researchers to probe further into the reasons for this revictimization.

Ken Pease and Gloria Laycock (1996) suggest that, beyond the characteristics of individuals and contexts, the victimization experience itself can increase risk. What they find is that an individual's past crime victimization is a good predictor of his or her subsequent victimization. So, while people with similar characteristics may experience different levels of victimization, the victim's experience of crime changes the odds that these individuals have for future vulnerability to crime. This finding is surprising given what we know about behavioral self-blame and the steps that people take to protect themselves after victimization. What the BCS data indicate is that repeat victimization occurs where the offsetting steps of prevention are harder to bring about. Higher revictimization occurs in crime-prone areas, repeats occur quickly after the prior occurrence, and the same offenders are involved. What this points to is what Pease and Laycock call a "hot dot," the victim who repeatedly suffers crime.

Put in risk terms, we would assume that, if someone had his or her home burglarized or was assaulted, robbed, or in some other way mistreated, the chances of this occurring again would be greatly reduced as the individual would make every effort to prevent it. While these actions may actually be taken, it appears that, despite this, the victimization recurs. Graham Farrell and Pease (1993) have suggested that this recurrence stems from factors in the environment over which the individual has little control, leaving exposure levels high. Or, intriguingly, there may be some characteristics of the individual that simply create a higher level of susceptibility to crime.

In puzzling out what might contribute to repeat victimization, Farrell, Coretta Phillips, and Pease (1995) suggest two possible explanations as to why it is that particular targets are more likely to be repeatedly involved in crime. The first explanation for repeat victimization is what they refer to as "risk heterogeneity." These authors explain that victims (or targets) have certain characteristics that increase the possibility that they will be victimized and victimized repeatedly. These characteristics are thought to exist prior to the initial victimization and are enduring, lasting both before and after initial and later victimizations.

A second explanation is "state dependence" (Farrell, Phillips, and Pease 1995, 386). State dependence refers to increasingly less effort on the part of the offender required to commit subsequent offenses, which may be due to postvictimization changes associated with the victim. Farrell and his colleagues note, "In the context of re-victimization presumed to be state-dependent, the basic question concerns reasons for the choice of the same [or different] perpetrators offending more than once against the same target[s] in preference to other targets" (386). Rather than enduring traits characterizing victims as in the previous explanation, state dependence implies that victimization changes victims to make them increasingly attractive. In other words, the likelihood of revictimization is potentially greater in the aftermath of an initial victimization than prior to initial victimization. Much of the psychological literature on victimization rests squarely within this perspective. For example, childhood sexual abuse is thought to impair the individual (i.e., in terms of evaluative judgment of hazard often via the onset of posttraumatic stress disorder), making the likelihood of adolescent and adult revictimization greater (Fergusson, Horwood, and Lynskey 1997; Koverola et al. 1996). Using the example of partner violence, Farrell and colleagues suggest that a single incident of victimization establishes for the offender the likelihood of guardianship. If the neighbors do not intervene in the violent incident or the police are not called, the offender perceives the likelihood of retribution to be increasingly unlikely with every subsequent offense, and the offender judges getting away with the crime as increasingly likely.

The National Center for Victims of Crime notes that women who have been assaulted in the past two years faced double the odds of a subsequent assault, while a subsequent assault for those who had been assaulted twice in the past two years quadrupled.[5] In sum, Farrell and colleagues (1995) note, "The obstacles to the repetition of partner assault are lower than its first occurrence" with every subsequent offense (387).

As a final note, there is an idea that appears to come from the public health literature that suggests that, if you reduce your personal risk, you reduce the risk to everyone around you. While this is based on a disease contagion model, the parallels are there in the context of the repeat crime victimization literature that suggests victimized individuals will be victimized again. If special attention is paid to reducing both their initial and subsequent victimizations, it is possible that the overall risk of crime goes down as other factors change (people sense greater security and act accordingly). Little attention has been paid to the importance of victim services in reducing overall crime rates—everything appears to have been focused on the reduction of targets,

but reduced crime rates might come about not only because of situation prevention but also because of the assistance that victims received in removing
them from subsequent crimes.

CRIME RATES (SPECIFIC/STATE)

We have shown that perception and fear can have strong influences on the
ways in which we respond to crime. Also, we discussed the importance of
victimization data in pointing to the susceptibility of certain groups to crime.
These statistics provide a basis upon which individuals define their risk of
victimization based on personal experience. As we have discussed, on a more
aggregate basis, law enforcement and policy makers rely more specifically on
direct measures of crime activity provided by crime rates.

In a review of crime statistics about thirty years ago, Michael Maltz (1975)
suggested at that time that there were three controversies plaguing the collection of crime data in the United States. The first had to do with the types
of data that should be collected. Maltz explains that the early decision was to
collect criminal court data, as that had the most complete information about
both crimes and offenders. On the other hand, arguments were made that the
most comprehensive measure of crime would be available from the police.
Thorsten Sellin argued that, the further away from the crime the data were recorded, the less value there is in the data—an argument for policing were over
and above court data (in Maltz 1977, 34). In the late 1960s and early 1970s,
victimization surveys came into play, suggesting that victimization was far
more common than crime data (as recorded by police) indicated.

A second issue concerned the agency responsible for collecting the data.
While individual agencies would be responsible for collecting their own
data, the overall compilation of the data would belong to the Uniform Crime
Reports (UCR), eventually housed with the FBI. A third issue had to do
with the accuracy of the statistics. Although data-collection methods have
improved somewhat since Maltz and others flagged this concern, issues of
accuracy, and more importantly, interpretation, continue to plague the use of
crime data.

A review by Gilbert Geis (1986) suggests that the meaning of crime data
is far from agreed upon. In 1985, the governor of California hosted a meeting with the participation of criminologists from across the United States.
That year, 1985, UCR data indicated a decrease in the levels of crime in the
United States. The commentary with regard to that decrease was cautious.
Not surprisingly, demographics figured into the discussion, with speculation
that changing demographics would result in overall declines in the crime rate.

(Others, as we noted earlier, suggested that teenage super-predators would wreak even greater havoc.) Attention was directed toward the geographic variations that still remained despite the decrease, as well as the variations in police practices and mandates that impact upon the recording of crime. It was further pointed out that different types of crime data tend to use different denominators and are therefore not comparable. A further issue (and one that we will consider more fully later in this book) was the danger of using past behavior as a means of predicting future behavior.

This is perhaps the most specific tie to the concept of risk that crime rates offer. They produce an image of crime both today and in the past—images that are a product of policing methods and processes. While crime rates are often used as a way of attempting to "harness the future"—making the future knowable—the difficulty is that crime rates are an artifact of policing. Other questions arose with respect to the nature of crime under consideration: white-collar crime, for example, was not included in the apparent decline. Geis concluded his overview with the suggestion that there are many factors that impact the crime rate and that crime is (and crime rates are) a by-product of the values that we hold in society.

HOT SPOTS (SPECIFIC/INSTITUTION)

Interestingly, the research on multiple victimization has also pointed to what is already well known in the criminology literature: crime takes place in specific, select areas, or "hot spots" (Sherman, Gartin, and Buerger 1989). Farrell and William Souza (2001) point out that individuals who are revictimized also tend to be located in these hot spots of crime. There is, therefore, a connection between the exposure that comes from being in high-crime-rate areas and the odds of the crime recurring that develops from being a victim. This takes on the character of the public health model that we talk about earlier (with respect to reducing crime probabilities for one party having the effect of reducing the probability of crime for all), but the increase in crime is not due to disease. Rather, it is due to the contamination effects of a concentration of large numbers of offenders in one location because of the attractiveness of certain areas for crime. Environmental criminologists have worked hard to explain the dynamics of crime concentration that has been facilitated in recent years by easy access to geographic-based crime data and the applications associated with sophisticated geographic information systems (GIS; see, in particular, Harries 1999).

The more recent work that has been done on crime hot spots returns us to the idea that certain areas are more likely to attract crime than are others

(Eck et al. 2005). The researchers who have studied these hot spots have asserted that crimes tend to group together, presumably because targets cluster together in certain locations. And yet, not much has been done to test whether these clusters are, in fact, target focused or are more likely to be due to other factors, such as the interaction effects that occur between social disorder (hazards) and offending. Areas of high social disorder are certainly not target rich in terms of property crime (although opportunity might be enhanced by lower guardianship).

What makes more sense is that when the risk of crime increases in a certain area, this impacts on the overall hazards. Specific targets may disappear, but the likelihood of crime intensifies. This is a function of the finding that, when there is an increased likelihood of success, there is less of a need to expend effort in committing a crime, and the presence of other crimes encourages future crimes. "Risky locations," those that harbor a greater likelihood of crime, signal this type of sequence. We can see this in the examples of prostitution strolls and drug markets. While we would expect that prostitution strolls would disappear because of strong police surveillance, they move but they don't disappear. Why is this?

It seems likely that they persist for a variety of reasons, but the convenience of location appears to be important. Prostitutes need clients, clients need to know where to find prostitutes, and the stroll needs to be located in an area in which the local residents are unable or unwilling to do anything about moving the activity. Further, the risk to those involved needs to be lower there than elsewhere. We find that certain areas exhibit a greater proportion of these designations that are functional to the completion of the criminal transaction. Drug markets develop based on locational determinants in much the same way. The probability of a negative outcome (being caught by authorities) cannot be completely removed from these transactions, but the markets provide easy access, reasonably secure environments, and a reduced likelihood of apprehension. Paradoxically, then, the clustering of these activities in certain "crime places" both increases the risk of crime occurrences and lowers the individual risk to participants.

Alison Ritter (2006) provides an excellent review of the many different ways in which we can look at drug markets: from an ethnographic point of view; using models of supply and demand; considering the psychological roots of these phenomena; evaluating public policy impacts; or looking at them using a criminological approach. She cites, in support of the criminological approach, two studies in particular that have examined drug markets as geospatial concentrations of illicit activity. The first, a study by Lorraine Mazerolle, Colleen Kadleck, and Jan Roehl (2004), considered the influence of police practice on drug markets and describes four different types of drug locations involving varying concentrations of a number of different factors that relate to social disorganization. These include calls for police service, commercial activity, and land use factors, such as length of the city block on which the behavior took place. This clustering of activity in particular areas is supported by the unique combination of these factors that support reduced detection, easy access, and so on.

The second study, by John Eck (1995), suggests that drug markets are formed through the development of a balance between the needs of buyers (in terms of access) and sellers (in terms of security). When these factors combine in certain ways, the propensity to create drug markets increases. A transition takes place from a lack of permanency of individual street sales to a more defined and stable location where an ongoing market emerges. Buyers know where to go to get the goods. Sellers know where to go to sell them. Distributors locate their stashes close to these places, and the police target them for enforcement. Drug markets are crime places that have a history and are likely to remain over time, despite the best efforts of the police to eradicate them.

Eck and David Weisburd (1995) offer an insightful overview of the theories that have addressed the conceptualization of crime places. "Specifically, we would want a theory that could tell us why certain targets are selected by offenders—why some targets are attractive and others are repellent. What are the impediments to offending that are presented to offenders and how are they overcome?" (4). Common to these environmentally based approaches is the view that opportunities for crime are not equally distributed across locations, nor are offenders successful in realizing opportunities given differences in the location and the guardianship that comes from surveillance of these locations.

In addressing clustering of incidents, Richard Block and Carolyn Block (1995) make a distinction between crime space and crime place. Space, they say, is an area forming the context or backdrop for place-level events. First, a space has attributes that are strictly area-level including, for example, population structure. Second, a space has attributes that represent an aggregate of place characteristics (which may include the number of buildings or land use in an area; Block and Block 1995, 148). This is consistent with the geographical view of space as representing physical structure in three-dimensional forms.

Place, according to Block and Block, includes the characteristics of individual locations (addresses, facilities, and building) and the cumulative effect when individual addresses are aggregated into spatial clusters (hot spot areas). They allude to the ecologists' interest in studying ecological processes in which "the whole is greater than the sum of its parts"—where the focus is on the potential or risk of crime in areas that comes as a result of the characteristics found in these areas.

As a caution, this type of analysis is subject to problems of what they refer to as "stationary fallacy," that is, an artificial clustering of events that actually occur at different time periods (Brantingham and Brantingham 1981). However, the advantage of this approach comes from providing evidence that crime events cluster spatially. Eck (2001) observes that the 10 percent of the places with the most crime accounts for about 60 percent of crime; that the 10 percent of the offenders committing the most crimes are involved in about 50 percent of the offenses; and that the 10 percent of the most victimized people are involved in about 40 percent of the crimes. As a consequence, repeat-address incidents dominate police work.

The identification of crime hot spots tells us where behavior is clustered, but connecting this to urban context has been a challenge for spatial analysis. Paul and Patricia Brantingham have helped us to understand these connections through the conceptualization of what they refer to as the "environmental backcloth" that emerges from the confluence of routine activities and physical structures overlaying urban areas. The Brantinghams (1995) suggest that this backcloth is dynamic and can be influenced by the forces of "crime attractors" and "crime generators." Attractors are what we would conventionally think of as crime spots that bring people to commit crime. Generators are based more on the creation of opportunities that come from the collection of people into areas with the crime problems occurring as a result of the increased volume of interaction taking place in these areas. Simply providing an overlay of urban facilities, socioeconomic characteristics, or transportation corridors creates an impression of interaction but fails to provide statistical support for these connections. The ideas of attractors and generators help us make this link.

The problem of the detachment of social characteristics and behavior has posed a challenge for urban researchers for decades. Researchers from the school of human ecology faced difficulties in asserting that certain neighborhood characteristics correlated with deviance in the face of the ecological fallacy that comes from connecting aggregate characteristics to individual behavior. When we commit the fallacy, we may decide, for example, that, because a neighborhood has a large concentration of a certain group, which we detect through census information that is compiled at the block face level, then members of this group are the ones committing crime. When we look at the actual incidents, however, we may find that the offenders are from a different group entirely who have come into a location to prey on local residents.

When the human ecologists began their study of the city of Chicago in the 1920s, their research was inspired by a search for patterns in urban form that was clearly identifiable and repeatable. In this quest, the researchers followed the lead of Robert Park, Roderick D. McKenzie, and Ernest Burgess (1925) in developing models or templates that could be superimposed on social behavior. The most important of these applications focused on the development of what the ecologists referred to as "natural areas," locations where people drawn from similar backgrounds congregated and pursued common interests. These natural areas were defined by boundaries that changed over time and developed, the ecologists argued, as a function of competition that led to selection processes that sorted groups from one another and allowed certain communities to win over others in the control of urban space. The ecologists, then, viewed urban change as a constant forming and re-forming of areas based on interactions between groups and competition over scarce resources.

In witnessing the changes that took place in cities such as Chicago, the ecologists further refined their analysis of natural areas by suggesting that competition for locations was influenced by the processes of invasion, succession, and segregation. These ecological factors had particularly strong impacts during the time of rapid immigration into urban areas, but the continuing effects of these processes can be witnessed today in the evolving character of ethnic communities in large cities.

Further refinement of the analytical approaches suggested by the ecologists was an effort to create models that transcended the experience of one city and captured the changes witnessed across all urban areas. The development of ideas, such as concentric zone or sector theories, provided the ecologists with tools to determine whether or not change followed prescribed patterns (in the case of the concentric zone theory the pattern of development from inner city to suburbs was predefined).

The ecologists had limited success in replicating their models, yet their explanation of urban change was compelling and has much currency even today. In particular, with the introduction of more sophisticated data-management systems and better individual-level data, researchers have much more opportunity to test ecological theories than was previously possible (Lo 2004). But the links between social structure and behavior remain an elusive empirical test.

Early efforts at making these connections were promoted in an important research initiative undertaken by Clifford Shaw and Henry McKay (1969). These researchers extended the ecological analysis to the study of crime and delinquency and collected data about urban neighborhoods in Chicago explicitly to identify where delinquency takes place. This research was groundbreaking at the time and predated much of the current work on hot spots that has since appeared in the criminology literature. However, while the search for clusters of delinquency was novel (it was not unprecedented as it appeared in the work of Charles Booth [1879] in his study of London in the nineteenth century), the Shaw and McKay work was actually much more important in its attempt to add temporal changes to the study of spatial distribution.

While crude in its approach, simply because both technology and data were limited, Shaw and McKay produced maps of Chicago neighborhoods reflecting three decades of data. In their analysis, they demonstrated that crime clustering occurred in similar locations over this time. They speculated that this occurred not because the same people committed these crimes but rather because these locations had enduring qualities that created opportunities for crime, regardless of who resided there. This argument for the enduring criminogenic neighborhood entered into the literature the idea that crime locations may have a repeatable form. At the same time, Shaw and McKay did not do much to explain why this occurred. They tried valiantly to explain the correlates of these types of outcomes. They persisted in the notion that crime and delinquency occur in context, not simply as a result of the presence of certain types of offenders.

It has only recently been the case that analysts have begun to look for interaction among elements in these environments—either interaction between crime incidents and locations or between actors and locations. The ecologists suggested rules for how interaction would take place in urban areas (Abbott 1997). Andrew Abbott argues that the ecologists' major task was to describe interactional fields. The renewed criminological interest in the Chicago perspective derives from a concern with spatial interdependence that reflects this interaction and the richness it brings to our understanding of social behavior.

As Abbott states, "The Chicago School thought that no social fact makes any sense abstracted from its context in social (and often geographic) space and social time. . . . Every social fact is situated, surrounded by other contextual facts and brought into being by a process relating it to past contexts" (1152). Abbott derides the efforts in contemporary urban studies to look for single causal factors. To him, the importance of the ecological approach was in its accounting of social interactions that occur in context (an empirical fact that was difficult to test, given the data and technology available at the time). He is critical of the efforts to use random sampling to generate survey respondents who would in turn produce individually based variables to be analyzed in terms of independent-dependent relationships, devoid of concerns about the social contexts in which characteristics are located and behaviors take place. While it is not clear that cross-sectional surveys restrict one's ability to look at context (see Kennedy and Baron 1993, for example), situational researchers have again turned attention to the contexts of crime and its locational dependence (see Wilcox, Land, and Hunt 2003).

Elizabeth Groff (2007), using advanced analytical techniques, has studied concentration effects of robbery and the physical landscape of the city using a simulation model that assesses the importance of time away from the home. She points out that, despite the emphasis on the changing character of crime opportunities because of shifts in activities, there has not been a concerted effort in the research literature to actually operationalize this opportunity shift, both in temporal and spatial terms. In her model, she shows that there are definite tendencies for crime to concentrate (as shown in much of the crime hot spots literature) but also to congregate in certain areas according to the structures of the underlying road patterns in the study areas. This is a particularly interesting observation, as it provides support for the notion that physical structure, as well as activity in public, will have an effect on the ways in which crime occurs. This seems to be a fairly obvious point, and one that has been imbedded in the research literature for some time, yet because of data problems and the complexity of the problem this relationship has been somewhat underappreciated.

George Tita and Elizabeth Griffiths (2005) take a slightly different approach focusing on the triangulation of crime, including victims, offenders, and locations of crime, in a way that allows us to better understand how proximity or difference might influence the likelihood of crime occurring (we also note the work done by Kim Rossmo [2000]; Ratcliffe [2006]; and George Rengert [1988] on these types of proximity effects).

We acknowledge the importance of clustering in developing patterns, but it is more than clustering that is taking place. This clustering appears to follow consistent rules. This is supported in the research reported by Pamela Roundtree and Kenneth Land (2000) where they studied multilevel models of burglary victimization across three cities. In their analysis, they conclude that victimization appears to take on similar forms in all cities in the same way. They make the point that this victimization is dependent on contextual effects that appear in these cities. Their findings provide some support for the idea that crimes such as burglary have their own spatial logic.

Can we sum this research up in risk terms? Does this concentration of incidents increase vulnerability and crime potential? Does this potential, in turn, translate into an overall climate of increased criminogenesis in particular areas? It may be that these crime places are self-generating, in the same way that victims are more likely than others (who have not been victimized) to be victimized again. The feedback mechanisms that reinforce the recurring pattern of crime may actually (as is the case with individual victimization) have an intensifying (or deflating) effect on subsequent events. The appearance of hot spots can be seen not simply as clustering but rather as fluctuating (intensifying) effects that come from the feedback of previous events. Attempts to control these fluctuating effects are part of the overall effort to reduce crime probability in favor of noncrime outcomes.

The natural areas of hot spots are self-reinforcing, self-defining, and self-regulating (there may be an upper limit to the frequency with which these events can occur). The interactions of actors and contexts are more important than the presence or absence of particular actors. What brings about intensifying effects and creates hot spots are social and natural boundaries. We can go further: These natural area hot spots have an identifiable form influenced by crime type. The context influences the recurring and repeatable form that we witness.

An equally intriguing phenomenon that has received little or no attention in the discussions about high-risk areas is the fact that certain locations, in close proximity to these hot spots, stay crime free. Surprisingly, despite being on the border of areas of social decline, there is little evidence of disorder in these crime-free areas. These areas sometimes benefit from natural boundaries, such as railroad lines or highways, but often there is simply a road to cross to move from one area to the next. The reasons for "cold spots" include the obvious, such as homeownership and active police patrol. But the less obvious factors seem to play as well. Again, the risk of disorder seems to decline if there is a strong investment in the community, either because it has strong ethnic group identification or because of highly involved residents who are committed to keeping their neighborhood vital and crime free. Robert Sampson and Stephen Raudenbush (1999) refer to this investment as social capital, or social (collective) efficacy (we talked about this earlier in discussing broken windows approaches), suggesting that the higher the capital, the lower the risk of disorder. This seems consistent with the opposite effect, lower capital leading to higher disorder, but the connection gets tangled in the discussions that have emerged about how these processes connect to crime. On the one hand, it is argued that raising capital decreases disorder that, in turn, reduces crime; the other promotes the view that reducing disorder reduces crime that, in turn, increases capital. While this calculation may seem to lead to the same outcome, the tactics in making changes in these areas are quite different depending on the view that is followed.

First, if we start with capital, the process requires that individuals and businesses expose themselves (in ways that may not be acceptable to them) to potential loss by investing capital in the face of the disorder spiral they believe they confront. The decisions that have been taken by governments to invest in redevelopment plans have had some success, particularly in areas where efforts have been made to replace derelict housing with higher-quality homes. However, the effects of these investments are slow and connect to greater probabilities of negative outcomes to start with; over time, these probabilities may begin to work in favor of positive outcomes.

Alternatively, if we start by reducing disorder, in particular, clamping down on minor offenses, the decision to alter police resources to target these crimes may result in other problems in other areas being untended. We also run the risk of having this form of policing create a backlash in the relationship of the police to the community, as quality of life policing can be more intrusive in the daily lives of the public. But the quality of life approach encourages collective risk taking that can then lead to greater private investment as the areas become more secure.

Seen in these terms, the question arises again: what factors lead the police to say they are successful in their interventions in tackling various social problems (or, alternatively, what evidence leads their critics to argue that they are not successful) and encourage residents to stay put and others to invest in a community's turnaround?

SCRIPTS (SPECIFIC/INDIVIDUAL)

When we move to the level of individuals in the transaction part of the crime event, we find that the focus on the straight cause/effect relationship we have discussed above begins to change. Instead, researchers who have looked at this stage suggest that the best way to understand what occurs here is to see it operating in terms of a transaction or interaction. On the surface, these transactions appear to evolve in rather random ways, as the individuals may not have a clear understanding of how the interaction will end up. However, analysts suggest that, while the outcomes may appear indeterminate, the participants actually follow clearly defined scripts that govern their behavior, manage the interactions, and portend the end result. Famous for his focus on interactions, Erving Goffman (1959) talked about the "presentation of self in everyday life" as a drama unfolding, with different actors following parts learned from others over time, resulting in an ongoing understanding of how others involved in the interaction interpret the meaning of the exchange. Goffman's insights led to the important observation that we need not always understand why individuals behave the way they do, that is, what motivates their behavior, provided we are aware of the rules they follow in guiding their actions.

The "interactionist" approach has been helpful in understanding how people learn, raise children, conduct business, and so on. It has also been applied in studies of how people manage conflict, including conflict that escalates to violence. In a landmark study of conflict, David Luckenbill and Daniel Doyle (1989) looked at the ways in which people caught up in violent events described the exchange leading to physical attack (even though, as they note, it may not have been apparent at the beginning of the conflict that violence would erupt). Luckenbill and Doyle suggest that we can understand this conflict by breaking the interaction into stages of "disputatiousness," each one defining how the interaction is then carried to the next level. The stages include "naming," "blaming," and "claiming." In the "naming," or beginning stage, the individuals define a conflict as having little consequence to them and they may break off the interaction. Or, they might argue that the other in the interaction in some way offended or insulted him or her. If this first stage escalates, it then moves to the blaming stage where the individuals identify who is at fault. Progressing from this stage, there is a "claim" made, perhaps involving a request for an apology or leading to a direct attack on the other (either in retaliation or revenge).

Leslie Kennedy and David Forde (1999) explore these conflict stages in great detail, looking at the conditions under which these types of conflict scripts would be enacted, leading to an escalation to violence. They suggest that, in cases where there is some ambivalence about claims or where there is a refusal to conciliate the argument, individuals will resort to more extreme measures. Of course, it is not surprising that these choices will vary according to age and gender of the individual parties and the age and gender mix in the groupings that are formed.

In looking at these scripts for conflict, a judgment is made about the claim based on the individual's own assessment of its justification, but there is also a decision to be made about the harm that might be done should retribution fail. In their interesting studies on violence among men, James Tedeschi and Richard Felson (1994) suggest there are important differences that appear in violent encounters depending on the size and weight differentials of the combatants. Now, this should not be surprising: You don't want to take on a fight that you are inevitably going to lose. At the same time, when the odds are seemingly equal, we find there are a number of things that might change the reasoning of the individuals to encourage or discourage them from entering into violence. This suggests that the risk calculation is not necessarily a strictly objective assessment of ability to "win" the conflict. A number of other factors come into play: status, insult, retribution, revenge, and honor. The distortion of the risk calculation by these factors does not make it less important; it simply suggests that, to understand it more completely, we need to see it in terms of the contexts in which these interactions take place.

In terms of actions that we would judge as risky if we were to look at them in "objective" terms alone, we note some interesting outcomes. Attacks between gang members due to insults triggering deadly responses would appear to fit the category that, "objectively," we would view as distorted (see also Osgood and Anderson [2004] on the effect of unstructured relations among juveniles in effecting the emergence of certain types of delinquent behavior). Equally, decisions made by individuals who have been previously victimized in a relationship (domestic or otherwise) to stay in their violent relationship appear to observers as increasing the possibility of future victimization. It is only when we understand context and the difficulty that individuals have in breaking away from defined scripts and situations that we can anticipate that they might be able to avoid this harmful behavior. This is complex as the risk calculation is deeply imbedded in the learned behavior of scripts. Although scripts appear to be rehearsed alone, their "success" is dependent upon the participation of other actors in them. Escaping this programmatic response can be daunting, and the determination to switch scripts may, at times, result in even greater exposure to harm, such as when women try to leave violent relationships leading to even more violence.

In understanding how probabilities of certain types of social interactions stay relatively constant over time, we need to return to the idea that certain individuals consistently follow risky lifestyles that expose them to crime, a point raised earlier when we talked about situational crime prevention. But the lifestyle itself may not be the contributing factor. Rather, the ongoing, continuous routine that is followed provides a repertoire of justification and support for following these behaviors. In an inspired article published by Robert Agnew (2006), he suggests that the routines of offenders are supported by their personal narratives, justifying and instructing their criminal behaviors. In explicating these narratives, individuals define the risks that they take, the costs of their behavior, and the reasons for them to continue, despite detection and punishment. In articulating and justifying these risks, the offenders provide an individual calculus for their behavior that provides support for their continued delinquent acts. Agnew even goes so far as to say that, in certain circumstances, the narratives themselves cause crime to happen, as offenders use the story line to justify their ongoing delinquent behavior. The offenders rationalize, minimizing the risk to themselves and dismissing, as limited, the harm that it does to others. In these stories, getting caught figures into the equation, but this can be seen as an unwelcome consequence of sometimes misjudging the risk.

So, we can see that a number of factors appear to play a role in the risk-taking stance of offenders. The judgment about apprehension and punishment (the costs of making an incorrect decision about the risk of committing a crime) is influenced by self-control, routines, justifications, available targets, and calculation of likely reward. It can also be impacted by the social conditions in which individuals find themselves, including the actions of others in the community and of social control agencies seeking to discourage the offender from acting (as is proposed in the Operation Ceasefire program). In considering the offender, then, we see that particular factors exert pressure on his or her actions. This coincides with the propensities of victims who come to crime events with a different set of calculations about what to expect and how to avoid harm.

It could be, however, that there is an interaction effect that develops in a way that both the choice of offenders and pressures from societal factors influence crime outcomes. This interaction has been discussed by Baron, Forde, and Kennedy (2007) in their study of the deviant lifestyles of male street youths. The authors show that exposure to conflict and the interactional dynamics of disputes lead to violence and victimization. Fueled by drugs, pressure from peers, and values that promote conflict, these youth view violence as a legitimate way to resolve conflicts. Interestingly enough, in these cases, it is sometimes hard to distinguish the offenders from the victims as both are drawn from this same group of combatants.

SUMMING UP

In this chapter, we deal with the general to specific aspects of risk of crime occurrence, looking at factors that influence crime rates, crime propensity, intelligence, crime hot spots, and victimization. We have shown that many different conditions are connected to the risk in crime, with the underlying theme in the crime literature focusing on the patterned responses that appear in creating crime propensity. Not surprisingly, criminologists have sought ways to document these patterns and have identified them at the state, neighborhood, and local levels. These patterns are surprisingly resilient, with variations that appear based on changing demographics, economic factors, or shifts in law enforcement practices. The patterns are also subject to influence from popular opinion or concerns that emerge, making some factors more salient than others.

We also see, in this discussion, the importance of the interaction between the risk evaluations of offenders, victims, and agencies of social control. These assessments do not operate in isolation from one another but are very much dependent on one another. Also, the experiences of crime (or the witnessing of crime events) can have important effects on individuals' future actions as we see in the altering risk profile that accompanies multiple victimization.

With these insights into the factors that connect to the actual incidence of crime, we now turn our attention to the crime aftermath to examine how risk plays a role in the reaction and response to criminal actions.

NOTES

1. We thank Norm Samuels for this observation.

2. Justice Information Sharing, "Fusion Centers and Intelligence Sharing," U.S. Department of Justice, Office of Justice Programs, 2008, at www.it.ojp.gov/default .aspx?area=nationalInitiatives&page=1181 (accessed June 2009).

3. Campbell Collaboration, "The Campbell Collaboration: What Helps? What Harms? Based on What Evidence," at www.campbellcollaboration.org/ (accessed July 2008).

4. Bureau of Justice Statistics, "Four Measures of Serious Violent Crime," U.S. Department of Justice, Office of Justice Programs, 2006, at www.ojp.usdoj.gov/bjs/ glance/tables/4meastab.htm (accessed June 2009).

5. National Center for Victims of Crime, "Repeat Victimization," at www .ncvc.org/ncvc/AGP.Net/Components/documentViewer/Download.aspxnz? DocumentID=41161 (accessed July 2008).

4

The Aftermath

LOOKING BACK TO SEE THE FUTURE

The familiar adage "hindsight is perfect" plays a large role in crime theories that attempt to explain current crime situations, as well as crime theories that hope to predict future crime events or crime levels. The idea of "looking back" to gather answers about current events is commonly used by the media and is frequently used by many of us to make sense of the world. We have become familiar with shows such as *CSI* (Crime Scene Investigation): armed forensics experts gather clues in order to identify suspects through evidence gleaned from minute details, often suggesting that certain "types" of offenders commit certain types of crimes. The idea promoted in these programs is that knowledge from the past—what certain types of offenders have done, their personal characteristics, whom they have previously victimized—can be used to answer questions about the present and the future.

While fictionalized accounts of explaining and solving crimes make use of historical factors, the practice is not limited to fiction. "Profiling," predicting crime involvement based on a variety of personal and social characteristics, along with characteristics of crime scenes, has enjoyed a fairly lengthy history in policing. Beyond individual-level predictions, policing agencies and crime analysts also make use of crime trends in order to predict future levels of crime: past crime rates are used to predict future crime rates. The idea is that, under conditions that appear roughly the same, we can expect that approximately the same crime rates will prevail (adjusting, perhaps, for population growth). The notion of "looking back" is also evident in new tools that have arrived on the policing scene to help policing organizations determine how and where they should allocate resources. Police are often under pressure to maximize limited resources. Applying their assets to areas that have a history of problems may be more effective than a blanket approach to addressing crime.

The idea of looking back at crimes already committed encourages us to make use of the data we have at hand to explain why crime events occur in the first place. At least part of the goal in looking back, however, is to not only explain what happened but also offer up clues and predictions of future events—looking forward, in other words, with a view to preventing crime. Perhaps the concept most clearly associated with looking both backward and forward is "deterrence"—an idea that comes from the realm of punishment. Deterrence refers to either threats of or actual retaliation or punishment as responses to particular behaviors. For example, we expect to be able to control behavior by warning would-be speeders that parts of the road are observed by cameras ready to note license plates (and issue tickets) to speeding drivers. The sign serves as a deterrent, or a threat, of a particular consequence to the act of speeding. If the driver proceeds to speed through the area, a ticket will result. Beyond the warning, the issuing of the ticket is also meant to serve as a deterrent—the behavior, speeding, is met with an unpleasant consequence or punishment. Presumably, wanting to avoid future tickets (punishment) persuades drivers to abide by the speed limit. Of course, tickets must be large enough to serve as a deterrent to drivers: if the consequence or punishment is "inconsequential"—the ticket amount is too small to warrant a change in behavior—there is little deterrence. As one could guess, the deterrent value of various threats depends upon a number of factors but also depends upon the type of behavior deterrents attempt to control—some forms of behavior are easier to control through deterrents than are others.

Once a crime or crimes have been committed, how do we respond? Punishment theory dictates that we may both redress the harm caused and respond in ways that prevent the same thing from happening again. There is a wide range of responses to the commission of crime. We will see that, despite the adage, hindsight is not as perfect as we often hope for. In looking back, we tend to make the often false assumption that there is a linear path between temporally distant points: point A (time 1), leads to point B (time 2), leads to point C (time 3), and so forth. Looking back at the past as a means of addressing the present and the future does not often adequately take into account the contingencies that may derail otherwise neat linear progressions between points, as well as the fact that it is often less-than-rational human beings who commit crime and are victimized by it.

CRIME TRENDS AND STATISTICS (GENERAL/STATE)

This speculation about the characteristics of crime rates and how they are impacted is a long-standing one. During the 1830s, European thinkers were especially concerned with "knowing" society through the collection of data about its citizenry. Information on individuals was collected and ranged widely from information on births, differences between males and females, marriages, deaths, residence, taxes, hospitals, time of year, physical stature, strength, pulse, and respiration, to name a few. Following this approach, Adolphe Quetelet (1842) applied probability theory to the study of crime behavior. What struck him at the time of his writing was the steadiness with which crime occurred, changing only marginally up and down, from year to year.[1]

Quetelet's efforts, which he referred to as "social physics," involved the practice of observation and measurement. He explained that facts were there for the observing; society simply had to take note of their existence. Rather than suggesting that theory lead observation, he believed that reason (theory) had to accommodate to the facts of the social world. Quetelet's analyses were not meant to explain the actions of individuals but instead resulted in averages. For example, Quetelet (1842) found that, on average, "the maximum energy of the passions occurs at about age 25" (ix). In other words, the height of criminal activity, for those who commit crime, is, on average, twenty-five years of age. Quetelet is careful to explain that this age cannot be applied to a specific individual—we cannot know that any specific person will commit the greatest amount of crime at age twenty-five. Quetelet's confidence in his observations, however, was apparent as he suggested that his "tables of criminality" for various ages could be regarded with as much faith as his "tables of mortality." While one could not determine one's exact age of death, one could see average life expectancies.

Quetelet is often referred to as a founding father of statistics. In particular, it was his use of data that earned him a reputation as being far ahead of his statistically inclined peers. Quetelet used the reams of data he compiled to determine the characteristics of the "average man." He explains that the data he collected (the observations) are each akin to an arrow aimed at a particular target. The arrows tend to cluster around the midpoint, but none may actually hit the center point itself. He suggests that, even though none of the arrows may hit the target dead center, the clustering of the arrows around the center in fact mark the center point—we can identify the center by the markings made by the arrows surrounding it.

Theodore Porter (1995) notes that Quetelet may have been particularly concerned with statistical laws because of living through a time of great social instability—the industrial revolution—with his observations providing some evidence of patterns despite social change. While the "average man" that Quetelet made famous actually applies to no specific individual (just as the "target" may never be hit), the average man is indeed socially produced as it represents a regularity of the social world. Porter explains that the significance of Quetelet's observation of crime rates is that, rather than patterns implying individual responsibility for crime, crimes rates instead suggest that crime may be social.

One of the patterns that Quetelet had predicted, that crime rates were relatively constant, was in fact borne out by the crime figures for the period from about 1857 to 1925 for England and Wales. The steady state of the crime figures was surprising, given that the police forces during this period doubled, and the population also grew. Howard Taylor (1998) explains the constancy in terms of "supply side" policies. What he means by this is that the supply of crimes was limited due to the means by which crimes were to be dealt with. He quotes from a barrister to the Royal Commission who states, "The punishment of every crime that is committed is clearly unattainable . . . the only attainable object is example" (572). For police officers, this meant that there was little use in recording much crime, as it would not be processed. Support for prosecutors was greatly diminished, and prosecution was seen as unnecessary. Taylor considered homicide statistics even more closely—homicides would unlikely be influenced by bureaucratic and political issues. In fact, Taylor found that homicides were also influenced by politics and suggested that "prosecutions for murder were among the most strictly rationed of all crimes" (585). Rather than the number of homicides fluctuating as might be expected, homicides were very expensive to investigate and prosecute. Because of this, cases that may have been somewhat trickier to establish, such as murder, were counted as other sorts of crimes or occurrences. As Taylor points out, while murders appeared relatively constant over the period from about 1860 to 1940, other forms of violent death were comparatively high (587). For example, suspicious deaths that lacked evidence were recorded as "suicide" or "accident," or even "suspicious death," which tended to be unencumbered by significant investigation.

Quetelet drew the conclusion that, although individual circumstances can create unpredictability in setting a trajectory for crime, overall rates of crime stay constant over time because of the determining factors of poverty, disorder, and inequality (the average man and the propensity to crime). This observation of relative stability in crime rates was actually considered quite a breakthrough at the time as the general belief was that crime occurred according to the random influences of evil, and crime was not patterned or predictable. Unfortunately, the debate around the statistical likelihood of fairly constant crime behavior committed by a small proportion of the population got lost in a subsequent debate around the morality of those committing the crime (see Beirne and Messerschmidt 2000).

Despite this diversion, Quetelet's observations about the constancy in crime rates over time underline the importance of probability in our understanding of overall risk. As we have said before, probability suggests that we can, with some confidence, predict outcomes in the behavior we are studying. There is an assumption in probability studies that, if all things stay equal, we would witness in the future what we have seen in the past. If certain things change, this may lead to different outcomes. The task of the criminologist is to correctly identify not simply factors that change but also factors that have a meaningful or significant impact on crime. These efforts to identify factors that impact crime are part of the effort to manage crime risk. Understanding what influences these outcomes is an important focus of crime analysis.

As for the distinction between individual-level risk and community-level factors impacting crime, there is a great deal of disagreement. This was evident in Quetelet's time and afterward, and involved much debate over the driving forces behind crime. The debates swirled around whether or not individuals had specific propensities to commit crime (set against a moral standard), based on social deficiencies, or whether or not they simply responded to underlying laws of social processes dictating that a certain number of crimes would occur each year, by chance, and the individuals simply obliged (see Menard [2001] for a discussion of the place of Quetelet in the general debate about the role of probability in influencing social outcomes). In the end, we needn't choose between community versus individual factors in establishing the probability of criminal outcomes but can and should look at both. Even with the careful scrutiny given to criminal careers by researchers looking at individual propensities to crime, there is an acknowledgment that entry into and exit from these careers can be influenced by penal policies (Blumstein and Cohen 1987). The likelihood of individuals turning to crime based on a life trajectory would seem at least partially contingent on the array of factors that evolve over time in larger society, putting social, economic, and political pressures on individuals and potentially increasing the likelihood of crime.

While the recording of crime has always been subject to various inter-pretations and agendas, the values we hold and how this impacts crime rates is taken up by Justin Baer and William Chambliss in a 1997 article entitled "Generating Fear: The Politics of Crime Reporting." These authors suggest that crime rates are suspect on a number of levels. First, the way in which crimes are counted in the United States means that crimes may be overcounted. Baer and Chambliss explain that the discovery of a body that appears to have been the result of murder is counted as a murder, even if evidence uncovered the next day determines that the death was due to accident. These authors explain that other countries will, by default, have much lower homicide rates because data are adjusted as information comes in. Similarly, different jurisdictions within the United States may count crimes according to the number of victims rather than incidents. (Say, for example, one person assaults many in a bar fight—the number of assaults will equal the number of victims, not the one incident.) Other parts of the criminal justice system, prosecutors and the courts, similarly contribute to the confusion surrounding crime rates. Rather than a crime being determined by the conviction, the crime is counted as it was charged. Police officers may attempt to upgrade charges by laying the most serious charge, while in court, plea bargaining and evidence only stand up to a downgraded charge.

The fluidity of crime rates is also called into question by Baer and Chambliss who cite studies of strategic manipulation of crime rates by the police who are able to force crime rates up or down. Citing the well-known case in the 1990s of the decreasing crime rates observed under Mayor Rudolph Giuliani in New York City, Baer and Chambliss note the downward pressures that were placed on precinct commanders to lower the crime rate. These authors also note that, during the 1990s, the trend was to point toward the increasing participation of juveniles in crime, as we pointed out earlier—despite the demographic trend showing declines in the proportion of the population that tend to commit crime. Rather than youth committing increasingly more crimes, the data have shown that youth levels remain proportionate to their size of the population.

Beyond the difficulties associated with the Uniform Crime Reports (UCR), Baer and Chambliss suggest that victimization surveys also tend to paint a picture of crime that is inaccurate. For example, when asked to report crimes of violence, response categories in the National Crime Victimization Survey include a range of offenses, from aggravated assaults and rape to attempts or threats of violence. However, when the data are reported as crimes of violence, they tend not to be separated in terms of completed offenses and attempts. By failing to separate completions and attempts, and failing to separate the more serious offenses from the less serious, a picture of "violent" victimization may be painted that fails to address the experience of most of those who have been victimized. Baer and Chambliss (1997) note that there is a "systemic bias in summarizing findings to make the frequency and seriousness of crime appear much worse than it is in fact" (102).

The goal when considering crime data is often to determine, from what has happened, what is likely to emerge. Again, we look to history as a means of explaining what we see today, and what we can expect for the future. Although drawing on the notion of hindsight, we see that there are difficulties with relying too much on historical trends. First, interpretations of what has occurred in the past are variable—do crime statistics tell a true story, or do they tell a story that is conjured in particular ways to suit political ends? If we find that crime rates have been "worked" in particular ways, on what basis can we translate these figures to produce policies to reduce the future commission of crime? As Quetelet reminded us some years ago, statistics may point toward the experiences of the "average man," but the average man, much like the gathering of data points that we see in crime trends, remains an elusive abstraction.

Quetelet's early observations about the stability of crime rates points to crime data as being a critical source of information with regard to efforts to manage crime risk. Given the many ways in which data can be manipulated, however, understanding precisely how and why data have been collected and coded is central. Given the manipulations that can occur, we see the importance of crime data in the way crime risk management is perceived. From the abstractions of crime data and crime trends that are the basis upon which policies are built, we turn now to general crime threats that pervade the institutional level. What can police do to reconcile the past with their present and future activities and their ability to deal with crime?

THE STORY OF COMPSTAT (GENERAL/INSTITUTION)

The police are charged with protecting the public, but their success at accomplishing this goal may depend on the measures employed to gauge success. One success story frequently cited in the academic literature and public news is the story of New York City and the radical drop in the crime rate evidenced during the second half of the 1990s. As we explained in chapter 1, the introduction of the new data-based accountability programs, such as CompStat, had a dramatic effect in changing the ways in which police did their business. The idea was that, rather than spread resources thinly across the New York City landscape, resources would be applied more directly to areas and problems that were revealed by the data as requiring specific attention through computerized reports of crimes in various locations. By focusing attention on high-crime areas, the crime should eventually go down because of the deterrent effects of heightened police presence and action. Although crime data were generated in the aftermath of its occurrence, the data compiled through analyses of past events would be used to address anticipated threats. In the discussion that follows, we expand our earlier discussion to consider the assumptions underlying the use of policing information, in general, and CompStat, in particular.

As noted by Paul O'Connell (2003) and William Bratton and Peter Knobler (1998), four principles underlie CompStat:

1. accurate and timely information;
2. rapid deployment;
3. effective tactics; and
4. follow-up and assessment.

Prior to considering these principles, let us discuss the larger idea behind efforts to make policing more efficient—the rationalization of the policing enterprise.

While the idea of using information and problem solving to guide policing decisions is not new, the idea has been put into practice less often than one might expect. Traditional policing could be described as driven by a military model of control, with information flowing down the chain of command and less information flowing from the rank and file upward. Increasingly, policing agencies became bureaucratized, with a culture that has tended to place greater emphasis on processes and policies than on substantive outcomes, such as the reduction of crime. This emphasis on procedures meant that line officers were becoming less responsive to their clientele—the public—and more concerned with maintaining bureaucratic rules. To counter this trend, as explained by former New York Police Department commissioner William Bratton, the idea was to develop a system that would address this kind of bureaucratic dysfunction and provide more people throughout the police agency with more information to make decisions.

In their study of the implementation of CompStat across a number of policing organizations, James Willis, Stephen Mastrofski, and David Weisburd (2003) suggest that, beyond the four principles mentioned above, six elements are central to the development of CompStat programs. These include

1. mission clarification, ensuring that members of the bureaucracy are "on the same page" with regard to what it is that the organization is doing;
2. internal accountability: the focus is on measurable results and clear reduction of problems within one's command;
3. geographical organization of operations, in contrast to central organization;
4. organizational flexibility, which refers to the ability to organize resources as problems come along;
5. using statistics and information to guide priorities; and
6. innovation as a feature to be rewarded while encouraging experimentation.

CompStat relates specifically to risk management and the ways in which the past (crimes committed and police responses to these crimes) can feed into how the police organize themselves to respond to future incidents of crime, as well as to prevent crimes from occurring in the first place. Having said that, initiatives implemented to combat bureaucratic dysfunction face a number of challenges. A key challenge is that bureaucratic structures tend to work within environments that are perceived as steady state—bureaucratic processes are developed that address what has occurred in the past, but they often do little to address what may occur in the future (Willis, Mastrofski, and Weisburd 2003). Bureaucracies are efficient if conditions stay the same—they are less able to navigate situations that fall outside the framework of tradition. Framed as a means of fighting crime, which is how police officers have traditionally viewed themselves (as crime fighters), CompStat aligns well with this view.

Willis and colleagues found, for example, that CompStat was perceived by officers as a means of doing better what they were supposed to be doing or clarifying their mission: fighting crime. The notion of internal accountability associated with CompStat, however, may not address bureaucratic dysfunction. The idea behind internal accountability is that responsibility for action is found throughout the bureaucratic structure. Rather than a top-down approach to addressing issues that arise, CompStat was expected to redistribute accountability throughout the structure. Given the traditional hierarchical structure of policing agencies, the redistribution of accountability may instead tend to reinforce the hierarchy with goals set by the top echelon of the organization. While responsibility for carrying out various practices may be found throughout, if top administrators are solely responsible for setting organizational objectives, the structure will not be a departure from the way in which accountability has been traditionally organized. Internal accountability also relates to organizational flexibility and to innovation. If the accountability structures that accompany CompStat duplicate or parallel traditional forms of organization, then the ability to innovate will be hampered, as will the ability to engage in flexible approaches to issues that arise. Failure, as Willis and colleagues note, is a part of innovation, but failure is not necessarily easily accepted in the face of particular accountability structures.

The use of data is clearly the key as CompStat, in particular, and intelligence-led policing more broadly, address bureaucratic dysfunction and may competently embrace policing challenges in the twenty-first century. As David Bayley (2008) and other policing experts have noted, the pressures on police come from all directions. However, it is their proximity to the scene of the crime, so to speak, that puts them in a position of power relative to others when it comes to collecting data related to the commission of crime—regardless of whether any charges are ever laid. Clearly, as we have discussed, victimization surveys paint a specific picture that is different than what policing data paint. But even with victimization surveys, various lenses of interpretation by victims and surveys influence how it is that victims define their experiences. Calls for service, for example, enable a wide variety of data to be recorded about crime, loosely defined (as only a relatively small proportion of the calls for service actually results in charges or any kind of criminal justice processing). The ability to acquire relatively raw data about crime and disorder places the police in the advantageous position of being keepers of data that a variety of other social control agencies may be able to and want to use. What CompStat encourages is using data to forecast: in other words, making use of data to predict where crimes might occur, and even to determine why crimes might occur. While policing agencies have collected data for a long time, it has less often been used as a method to drive decisions with regard to identifying causes of crime. In their study of the adoption of CompStat in Lowell, Massachusetts, Willis and his colleagues (2003) found that their observations were similar to the findings of others—crime analysis was not a priority, and relatively little work was done regarding the understanding of underlying causes of particular problem areas. Beginning to address the causes and predictors of crime, as Willis and colleagues note, will require a much different orientation toward data, including training in statistical methods of analysis.

At the institutional level, when facing nonspecific and abstract threats, one way of dealing with this sort of environment is to put into place policies and procedures that are flexible and less constrained by specific parameters of what has occurred in the past. This is particularly challenging, however, when knowing the future is based primarily on experiences from the past. We are reminded of the 9/11 Commission Report whose authors state that the procedures in place to deal with known threats were not the problem (Kean and Hamilton 2004). The problem, instead, was that the situation encountered on September 11, 2001, was not *imagined*. While clearly institutions cannot deal effectively with what can scarcely be imagined (including threats that are so abstract that they cannot be named), institutional responses can consider the knowledge they acquire through experience in ways that do not speak specifically to past practices. In other words, rather than simply categorizing events after they have occurred as being of one type or another, it may make more sense to look at how situations and crime events have differed over time. As Amos Tversky and Daniel Kahneman's (1981) notion of "representativeness" suggests, we tend to frame events in terms of what is known. We understand events according to the common features that situations engender. In contrast, abstract threat may require "pulling up the anchor" to a certain degree and enabling approaches that depend less on policies and procedures established in the past. CompStat may be one approach that can facilitate such flexibility, but the degree to which it can live up to its potential is in the hands of the institutions themselves.

PUNISHMENT

The concept of risk is perhaps nowhere more clearly evident than in our responses to crime: a hope we often have is that the way in which we respond to crime today will minimize the occurrence of crime in the future. Yet, responding to crime varies depending upon who or what is responding—whether responses emanate from individuals, institutions, or states—and the nature of the crime. Individuals, as we have noted, may ignore that a crime has occurred; they may avoid dealing with a crime situation; or they may report it. Individual responses to crimes are often influenced by what is at stake and how directly one is impacted by the crime. Institutional responses to offending may consist of alternative measures—including redirecting offenders from the criminal justice system entirely. Formal responses at the institutional level, which involve the courts and correctional systems, largely consist of rehabilitation, retribution or punishment, and restitution.

What is critical about the way in which we respond to crime is that we make assumptions about, first, the offender and, second, the crime itself. When considering how to respond to crime, we assess characteristics particular to the offender—what is the offender's mental capacity? What is his or her family background? Are there addiction issues? Is there a record of past offending? The idea behind looking at offender characteristics is that we need to establish if there is something specific to his or her background that has led to crime and if we can somehow reduce the probability that the offender will repeat the past.

On the other hand, we may determine that the crime was not prompted by any characteristic specific to the offender but rather that it may have been the outcome of specific situational prompts and cues. The offender, in other words, is not assumed to be suffering from any particular deficit outside the norm of what plagues others, and the crime instead becomes the focus. With an orientation focused on the crime, we see a greater emphasis on the action or behavior—the crime itself—rather than on the actor. In reality, our responses to crime are determined by some combination of characteristics of both offenders and their crimes.

Another key consideration when we respond to crime is the expectations we have of our decisions to respond in particular ways. For example, when offenders are sentenced to community service, pay a fine, or are sent to prison, what is it that we expect of that punishment? There are two orientations that ask us to address our expectations of punishment, the presence or absence of attention to consequence or consequentialism and nonconsequentialism. We turn first to the consequentialist perspective.

CONSEQUENTIALISM

Consequentialists argue that the rightfulness or wrongfulness of activity depends upon the outcomes associated with particular behaviors. For example, crime behavior is often seen as wrongful because it is harmful—harm is the result of crime activity (monetary, physical, or social harm). While responding to an initially harmful act with another harmful act (punishment) is problematic, punishment may be seen as justifiable given that the consequences of punishment are positive because some people are prevented from doing subsequent harm (committing crime). Punishment is therefore justified in terms of prevention. Although consequentialism typically concerns itself with the application of punishment, it is oriented toward the future and can include responses that fall outside the realm of punishment, including, for example, treatment and restitution.

This approach is often associated with a utilitarian perspective that considers whether various practices promote or destroy happiness, dominion, autonomy, or welfare (Duff and Garland 1994, 6). Importantly, these goods—happiness, dominion, and so on—can be achieved independent of punishment; punishment is not required for these outcomes, and other forms of responding can achieve the same ends. The ideas behind consequentialism are clearly associated with risk—responses today will either increase or decrease the probability that crimes will take place in the future. While offering the possibility of prevention, this perspective also speaks well to deterrence.

As mentioned at the outset of this chapter, deterrence specifically deals with responding to crime and how responses to crime (or perceptions of responses to crime) will redirect individuals from committing crime. There are two forms of deterrence, specific and general. The idea behind specific deterrence is that designated individuals are deterred from future criminal activity. An example of a specific deterrent might be incapacitating an individual, reducing his or her ability to continue to commit crimes—the prison walls deter future criminal activity. Another specific deterrent could involve an offender taking an anger-management program, with the expectation that the individual will be better able to control his or her anger and commit fewer offenses in the future. General deterrence, on the other hand, is about "messaging" and communicating to the general public that particular types of behaviors are unacceptable. We do not, for example, have to experience being thrown in jail to imagine that being thrown in jail is something we do not want to experience—we are deterred from committing crimes for which we know that a certain consequence (imprisonment) may result.

The Problem of Consequentialism and Risk

The late 1960s heralded a new penal discourse in opposition to "reformative ambitions" that had included punishment, but also treatment and rehabilitative programs, with the introduction of the "nothing works" discourse (Duff and Garland 1994, 8–9). The reasons for the disenchantment with reformative efforts included a shift in focus from the state to the individual and the emphasis on rationality as characteristic of offenders. Individual rights, including the rights of the offender, were highlighted. Prisoner's rights groups were on the rise, along with the idea that prisoners need protection from an overly intrusive state. Of specific concern was the fact that offenders appeared to have little say in the treatments and programs to which they would be subject. Forcing these programs on individuals violated their freedoms, according to the critics. A related issue is the differential treatment of individuals who committed similar crimes: individuals identified as high risk were treated differently from those who committed similar crimes but who were not categorized as high risk (with high-risk individuals characterized by particular demographic and social characteristics associated with a greater likelihood of offending). At issue was the predictive capacity of the various schemata used to determine who may reoffend based on past offending, which often produced a large number of false positives and false negatives. For example, some of those who were expected to reoffend given their histories did not reoffend; therefore, the model produced false positives. On the other hand, those who were not expected to offend did, in fact, reoffend, producing false negatives. As discussed earlier, differential treatment based on expected likelihood of reoffending proved to be inaccurate, resulting in some offenders being treated needlessly harshly (such as being defined as dangerous offenders or enduring severe punishment such as solitary confinement), while those who were not expected to offend, but eventually did, were treated comparatively leniently.

Central to the problem of prediction is the dilemma of moral responsibility and agency. Treating individuals in a particular way based upon what *might* happen or what could happen—how they may *potentially* behave—is problematic. We tend to assume that individuals are moral agents and can choose what they will or will not do. It is very problematic for the state or for institutions to respond to individuals as though a future possibility has already taken place. In other situations, such discriminatory practices are clearly not tolerated, for example, in the workplace, but appear with greater regularity in the realm of public security.[2]

The idea that individuals are able to choose a course of action refutes pigeonholing individuals for what they *might* do. Individuals are indeed capable of rational thought and are capable of exercising choice. The assumption of rationality is particularly problematic when it comes to deterrence. As we noted earlier, deterrence specifically addresses the future—deterrence is a means of controlling the future by making particular options for behavior appear unattractive (or, in some cases, impossible, as in the case of incarceration) by responding in specific ways. Underlying deterrence is the view that individuals will be able to rationally consider options and that they will also have the resources at hand to be able to learn about the consequences that specific actions entail—there is an assumption that citizens know the law. In the first instance, it is difficult to believe that an individual engaged in a street fight will take the time to think about the law and consequences of his or her actions in the heat of the moment.

In the case of general deterrence, there is an assumption that the general public takes into account the consequences of the past practices of others prior to committing a particular act. This further assumes that the public is aware of what happens in the aftermath of various crimes, regardless of who commits them. While we can imagine what they are, not many of us have a clear idea of the consequences of committing certain crimes, and it is difficult to assume we can learn from the experiences of others when it is not necessarily the case that we can even learn from our own experiences.

Related to learning from others is the idea that it is morally problematic for the state to respond to offenders with a view to using them to teach or show others how they must, in turn, behave. This idea is based on the Kantian claim that individuals should not be treated as "means," but must rather be viewed as "'ends." The idea behind general deterrence is that particular individuals are used to teach the rest of us, which unduly pressures these individuals into roles they have not asked to play but are playing independent of their own wishes.

NONCONSEQUENTIALISM

Perhaps the best way to describe nonconsequentialist approaches to dealing with crime is to see these as backward looking: punishment is viewed as the most relevant response to the commission of crime. Crime causes harm; harm should be the response to crime. This perspective supports retribution. Further, it is only the individual who must be punished—other parties' learning from this incident has nothing to do with the punishment. While it may be a fortunate outcome if, by administering a punishment, another individual is deterred from committing future crimes, the point is not to look to a specific future but instead to redress the offender's past crime. The point of punishing an individual who commits a crime is not to convey a deterrent message to others: the punishment must address the offender him- or herself, as "payment for the crime."

A key consideration in this perspective is the issue of proportionality—ensuring that the punishment fits the crime. Antony Duff and David Garland (1994) note that the link between the crime and punishment is that of "desert" and deservingness. The difficulty, however, lies not only in establishing what punishment fits the crime but also in the justification for the link between crime and pain: on what basis do we determine the appropriate response to crime?

Nonconsequentialists view retribution as central to responding to crime, but the connection between the crime and the response is not entirely clear. Arguments in favor of a retributivist response, however, suggest that the offender took an unfair advantage when committing a crime; therefore, the advantage gained must be taken back. Punishment takes back the advantage gained.

Duff and Garland (1994) suggest that today we find ourselves in a "retributivist revival" due, at least in part, to limitations in penal practice (12). The practicalities of offering individualized treatment are clearly beyond the scope of what can be offered to most of those who offend. Sentences that are handed out by the judiciary speak as well as they can to specific cases, not necessarily to particular philosophies, and sentences reflect the reality of what can be offered in any particular region. Not all regions have a wide scope of treatment facilities available, for example, and offenders may be placed in various facilities based more on vacancy than on programmatic offerings. Retribution may simply be all there is left.

Unfortunately, a retributivist philosophy and practice fit well in the current political context in a post-9/11 world. Rather than ensuring that we understand the range of potential reasons behind specific behaviors, the tendency now is to preempt possible behavior well in advance. In other words, rather than focusing on motivations, we focus on action (or possible action) and react in the same way to both action and its potential—an approach that is inherently backward looking. Zero tolerance is another example of preemptive strike. The cachet of zero tolerance is that it signals "uncompromising and authoritative action . . . against an external or internal enemy" (Newburn and Jones 2007, 223). Zero tolerance, therefore, aligns with a consequentialist perspective—punishing today to prohibit breaches tomorrow. The difficulty with zero tolerance, however, is that it does not look forward but instead looks back at the past and addresses what has occurred, more so than it can address what will occur.

Responding to crime is clearly a form of risk management, though the motivations to punish may not always be based on risk and crime probabilities, and may also be based on other perceptions of and orientations toward what has happened. At the same time, every response to criminal activity marks the beginning of other possible criminal events, so how we respond to what has occurred is critical to managing future occurrences. Responses to crime (and other behaviors) set up the future we create.

HATE CRIME (GENERAL/INDIVIDUAL)

In looking at consequences, we find that certain groups are more likely to endure both initial and repeated victimization. In assessing this risk, we see the influence of actuarial approaches to potential misfortune frequently applied, as in the case of vehicle insurance: young men tend to constitute the group that has a greater proportion of accidents. Insurance rates are therefore adjusted accordingly, with young men paying more for their premiums than do other groups. In the case of insurance, regardless of whether an individual within the group has had any accidents, the "record" tends to be applied to everyone belonging to that group in advance of accidents actually taking place. When we think of actuarial approaches as these apply to crime, we tend to similarly think of perpetration: some groups are more likely than others to perpetrate crime. As with accidents, young men tend to be more involved in crime (as both offenders and victims) than other groups. At the same time that certain groups are more likely to contain individuals who commit crime or have accidents, there are groups identified by others as having particular social and other characteristics that may cause them to be victimized at disproportionate rates. The disproportionate victimization of certain groups is referred to as bias-motivated or hate crime.

In her review of the literature, Kathleen Blee (2007) notes that most work on hate crime has been geared to identifying factors that contribute to how these incidents occur, how the authorities handle crimes identified as biased, and the characteristics of offenders who commit these types of crimes. But Blee alerts us to the fact that interpretations may differ among the group that has been targeted and victimized by these crimes—not all similarly identify the crimes that their group experiences as hate crime. Taking a step back from individual members' interpretations, in her analysis of an attack in Australia involving a group of offenders who targeted and killed gay men (referred to as the Snowtown event), Gail Mason suggests that society tends to acknowledge only certain victims as being hate crime victims and that the label of hate crime is subject to an emotional evaluation by those who consider the crime—both as formal and informal judges. This means that both individuals and society define the probability of (their own and others') victimization, and victimization itself, quite differently. Individuals who are placed in various categories by others find that these categories fail to describe their interpretations of the social world around them. Similarly, those who define themselves according to membership in these categories will interpret various experiences much differently than those standing outside of particular categories. In the discussion that follows, we consider Blee's findings from her study of the microdynamics of hate violence and then consider the Snowtown case and the importance of the emotional element in how we define particular types of crime.

Blee (2007) used a microhistorical method to study what she called "ethnoviolence." She describes this method as a means of understanding larger social processes by focusing on the detailed accounts of the lives of individuals participating in various social activities, at the same time prioritizing the importance of time and place to how understandings unfold. She studied both perpetrators and victims of ethnoviolence and found that both groups challenge our notions of who is at risk (or perceives themselves at risk) of offending or victimization.

Many of us might imagine that groups who commit various acts of ethnoviolence have come together because of being united in their hate-motivated ambitions. In contrast, Blee found that membership in hate groups may not be motivated at the outset by particularly strong feelings of animosity for the groups eventually attacked. Instead, Blee describes how racial superiority is introduced to potential members over the course of time, for example, during discussions about children's schooling or public violence. Animosity toward various races was the outcome of members' associations with other members—it wasn't a motivating factor that brought individuals together to form associations based upon a particular preexisting animus. Drawing upon historian Claudia Koonz's observation, Blee (2007) notes that "extreme outcomes are not always derived from extreme causes" (263).

Perhaps equally interesting is her observation that, rather than racial animus drawing groups together, it was individuals' attractions to violence that contributed to building racist groups. Blee (2007) found that, while many racist groups used violence strategically against targeted groups, violence itself was a source of attraction and was used against each other: "Racist activists also commonly attack each other, often viciously and with horrific consequences, and engage in and celebrate self-inflicted violence" (263). For those participating in these groups, violence was seen as a form of power, strength, and control—racism can be an outcome of this worldview, not only the other way around.

Turning to victims of hate crime, Blee notes that, not unlike other groups placed in other types of actuarial categories, hate crime victims do not interpret their experiences in similar ways: there may be numerous interpretations of what has transpired and what experiences mean for the future. As well as varying interpretations between victims and victim communities, interpretations change over time. In the eyes of the law, specific victimizations may be interpreted as hate crime if they meet certain criteria. Once labeled as hate crime, Blee notes, such labeling is relatively immutable. For victims, however, interpretations of crimes against them may contradict the official assessment of events. An example of this is when victims refuse to interpret arsons against mosques as being hate motivated but instead interpret these events as random. Other victims may come to define their experiences as hate motivated only after some time has passed. Differences in opinion about how crimes are interpreted tend to deepen divides within the group.

Group members also varied in terms of how they defined their victimization depending upon their individual standing in the larger communities in
which they reside: definitions and interpretations by individuals were sensitive to "victim enfranchisement." For example, Blee notes that, when a member of the victimized group feels him- or herself to be in good standing in the
community, especially those who are lawyers and doctors, for example, the
victimization is less likely to be defined as due to hate crime. Individuals who
do not have as much status, on the other hand, were more likely to define the
experience as a hate crime. In another context, workers who were the victims
of a variety of abuses interpreted their victimization as simply part of life and
not as racially motivated. Blee summarizes her observations by noting that
interpreting crimes is not simply a product of the types of acts committed or
the social standing of the victims. She asserts that "victims' interpretations of
the place of the violence in a sequence of acts of violence, the means whereby
they were chosen for victimization, the social groups and institutions through
which their claims are exerted, and their self-definition vis-à-vis a larger community of citizens are influential in this process" (Blee 2007, 266).

The policy implications of Blee's observations are significant. First, she
suggests that the potential for hate-motivated crime may be greater than first
thought. Individuals who claim not to have had preexisting racial animus became, over time, acculturated in groups that promote racist sentiments. This
means that the opportunities for acquiring members may be, in fact, quite
large. Further, this suggests that the likelihood or risk of this type of crime is
also larger than anticipated. Second, because attraction to and participation in
violence often led to hate-motivated crime, more attention should be paid to
those who are attracted to violence, as it may be the stepping stone to further
difficulties for and targeting of particular groups. Blee's third observation,
that not all members of a targeted group define their experiences in similar
ways and may define their experiences in ways that differ markedly from
how experiences are categorized by law, suggests that more attention should
be paid to the victimization of individuals that occurs outside the context of
legally defined hate crime, to incidents of "incivility," which may contribute
to feelings of fear and vulnerability. While these findings speak to how past
experiences contribute to abstract perceptions of threat, these observations
about hate crime suggest that individual interpretations of the past and subsequent perceptions of vulnerability after the fact are complex. For our purposes,
this means that, while history suggests that particular groups are more or
less prone to both offending and victimization, the ways in which individual
members of these groups perceive their membership in particular categories
and their vulnerability to future involvement in crime is very much dependent
on the social and historical contexts in which crime events are understood.

Mason explains that the ways in which society formally and informally responds to various crimes has a lot to do with the emotional responses associated with our perceptions of both offenders and victims. Drawing upon Nils Christie's notion of the "ideal victim"—a victim who is, by every measure, legitimate and unambiguous in terms of victim status—Mason suggests that the application of the label "hate crime" reflects qualities related to not only the motivations of offenders but also the characteristics of the victims. Beyond establishing that the offender was motivated by hatred, Mason explains that observers also require an emotional response to victims of crime. The naming and understanding of a crime as a hate crime is "dependent upon the likelihood that the event will generate forms of emotional thinking that are capable of coding its perpetrators as morally bankrupt and its victims as the undeserving objects of prejudice" (Mason 2007, 252). She argues that both emotional responses are necessary to result in the application of the label of hate crime and the understanding of the crime in such terms.

Drawing upon the Snowtown murder case that occurred during the 1990s in Australia, Mason considered both court transcripts and media reports of this event. The case involved the trial of two men who had been sentenced, respectively, with eleven and seven counts of murder. Victims were selected on the basis of the two men's antigay and antipedophilic hatred. While the court clearly defined these murders as motivated by hate, the representation by the media to the public was geared toward an understanding of the crime that undermined the likelihood of seeing the victims as ideal, and therefore the label "hate crime" was not applied. Due to the perceived characteristics of the victims, the victims did not generate the requisite compassion for such a label with the result that victims' groups also did not step up to support the notion that these crimes were hate crimes.

For crimes to be labeled as hate crime, Mason explains, the events must generate not only disgust for the perpetrators of the crimes but also compassion for the victims. Drawing upon the reports in the media, Mason (2007) observed that the victims were described in extremely negative ways: as living in a "sickening squalor and stench" and as being involved in "creepy incestuousness," reflecting that the victims and perpetrators came from the same socioeconomic realm and were known to each other (261). The victims were not clearly defined as different than their perpetrators, which in turn did not generate the compassion required to view the entire situation as morally reprehensible, as in the case of other hate crimes that generate disgust for offenders and compassion for victims. Mason observes that the murderers mistakenly linked homosexuality with pedophilia, while subsequent media reports did not necessarily undermine this link that had been drawn. While gays have deserved recognition as an oppressed group, pedophiles, on the other hand, "have never been seen as an oppressed group deserving of recognition or protected status" (263). The victims, in general, were painted by the media as having "deep moral failings" that undermined any sense of compassion for them. Rather than the identities of a specific group of victims generating compassion, as is the case for hate crime, the focus turned to the less morally charged framing of the event as a case of "serial murder." As Mason notes, "Serial killing makes no wider moral claim to improve the circumstances of those groups of people who are its primary victims" (265).

While the Snowtown case speaks to a specific situation involving a specific crime, it is important to consider the implications of this case for the ways in which categories or groups of individuals perceive abstract threats and the ways in which the public also acknowledges and supports claims by various groups regarding their (threatened or actual) victimization. Individuals who belong to certain groups may feel themselves to be generally threatened—the risk is not necessarily specific to a particular threat emanating from a particular source but may be pervasive. And yet clearly not every member of a targeted group has experienced victimization (as a result of group membership) directly. We are often placed into categories that undermine or bolster our claims of being threatened or victimized by virtue of such membership, which may, in turn, bolster or undermine our claims that "people like us" have been previously victimized by crime.

Both Blee's and Mason's analyses suggest that interpretations of and experiences with crime against one's group (whether that experience is direct or vicarious as a member of the group) are much more variable than previously imagined. The idea of victim enfranchisement suggests that abstract threats and concrete crimes are only more or less acknowledged by members of particular groups. Mason's analysis of the Snowtown crimes further suggests that membership in particular groups has much to do with the validation that particular groups (whether self-identified as such or not) will engender in the public realm.

In the discussion to this point, we have focused on crime threats in the abstract and how it is that such threats have been addressed in the aftermath of crimes having occurred. We see that there are difficulties at the state and institutional levels associated with addressing general or abstract threats of crime. Crime rates are clearly abstractions—we noted earlier that there is much concern over rates of crime, yet we also know that calculation of these rates can be influenced by a number of factors. Similarly, while programs such as CompStat are used to address abstract threats of crime, the way in which information is put to work is limited. We now turn our attention to specific threats of crime and the means by which states, institutions, and individuals address these specific threats in the aftermath of crime occurrences.

BORDER CONTROL (SPECIFIC/STATE)

In advance of traveling to our North American neighbors or overseas, we busy ourselves with ensuring we have the correct paperwork. Depending upon the nature of the visit—of which there must often be proof through the provision of details such as arrival details and itineraries—and the destination, we arm ourselves with passports, birth certificates, visas, return tickets, banking details, and immunization records. Rather than heralding an era that is borderless, as globalization once promised, we are asked to provide increasingly more proof of who we are and how we plan to spend our time in our host country and, importantly, when we plan to leave. Rather than debordering, William Walters, among others, refers to this as "rebordering," evidenced by the use of sophisticated surveillance equipment, large increases in operating budgets, and enhanced policing, to name a few. As Walters (2006) notes, borders are increasingly seen as "spaces and instruments for the policing of a variety of actors, objects and processes whose common denominator is their 'mobility'" (188). For example, specific threats may consist of people (drug dealers), their "stuff" (drugs), and the activities they wish to engage in (drug selling).

While we have tended to think of borders as gateways or boundaries between one state and another, borders are tending to increasingly exhibit remote control, whereby the locus of border activities has moved increasingly away from the border itself (Walters 2006, 193). For example, we get official word of our welcome into a country well in advance of approaching the border when we are issued travel visas or work permits. Our applications are accepted or denied before actual travel. Similarly, processes such as supply-chain management begin the process of crossing borders well in advance by planning and managing all elements of the supply chain. Suppliers who don't conform to these preparations at each stage of the process will be denied access to their destination. The effect of this form of management is that the "transportation system becomes a kind of networked border" (195).

In terms of policing borders, the key point is to prevent the entrance of what Peter Andreas (2003) refers to as "clandestine transnational actors" (or CTAs), defined as "nonstate actors who operate across national borders in violation of state laws and who attempt to evade law enforcement efforts" (78). Previously, the worry about the entrance of CTAs had to do with immigration and drugs. The United States has put a serious amount of money behind its efforts to control both migrants and the drug trade over the past thirty years. Clearly, the assumption from a border security perspective is that the threat emanates from outside, threatening to contaminate that within (see Douglas 1966). These efforts have included militaristic technology such as footfall detectors and infrared sensors along the U.S. southern border (Andreas 2003, 90). Since September 2001, however, perceptions of threat have changed from the drug trade and immigration to terrorism. Threats that come from the outside remain significant resulting in new bureaucratic policies meant to control CTAs. Andreas explains the difficulty: "The inescapable predicament facing border control strategists is that the massive volume of cross-border trade and travel requires that borders function not simply as barriers against CTAs, but as filters that do not impede legitimate border crossings" (92).

Border security amounts to the state's effort to reduce the likelihood that specific threats will be allowed to enter a country. Identified threats have varied over time, though Andreas (2003) argues that border control is now "about the policing of CTAs, with terrorists, drug traffickers, unauthorized migrants, and migrant smugglers leading the list of state targets" (107). He further explains the multiple functions of policing the border as vigorously as is done in the United States and Europe:

> Policing CTAs is not only about deterrence; it is also about projecting an image of moral resolve and propping up the state's territorial legitimacy. Everyday border control activities—checking travel documents, inspecting cargo and luggage, patrolling coastlines and airports, apprehending unauthorized entrants— are part of what gives the state an image of authority and power. (110)

States address specific threats through various border security methods, including profiling methods that anticipate that certain types of people will engage in wrongdoing, but also methods that draw specifically on the records of those who have committed various acts in the past. Similarly, on the domestic front, we have seen the development of profiling strategies that have been developed to manage (with a view to decreasing the likelihood of reoffending) and control sex offenders.

OFFENDER REGISTRIES (SPECIFIC/INSTITUTION)

In the discussion that follows, we highlight the difficulties associated with dealing with threats that are, for some, abstract, yet for others are concrete realities. For example, legislation often provides a set of guidelines meant to cover the wide range of activities included in more abstract, general scenarios. While legislation cannot be designed to address the specificities of each particular threat, we note the difficulties that arise because of distinctions between legislation and lived realities. Those who assess the likelihood of an individual's future involvement in crime—such as prison officials and probation officers—rely on scales and guidelines that are developed through repeated measures of (other) individuals in order to create norms and averages, but the degree to which these may apply to any particular individual is always in question. To add to this complication, the institutions that deal with particular issues—such as reoffending—may not define the likelihood of reoffending in similar ways.

We can now consider the problematic relationship between sex offenders and the public, both in terms of sex offender registries and offenders' release into communities. This discussion illustrates the tripartite tensions between institutions (both the criminal justice system and the police), the community, and threats or offenders. In the case of sex offender registries, for example, the source of threat is specific and known (individual offenders are identified) and sometimes contested (some agencies see these individuals as threats, others as nonthreatening), but the target of these particular threats is relatively indeterminate but seen as constant (consisting, largely, of women and children). Yet, targets are narrowed to specific geographic areas as per specific community notifications. Threats due to unknown offenders, who are a much larger group, are not addressed by these efforts. A further issue is that the threat sex offenders are presumed to pose is for crimes *previously* committed—predicting their future behavior is difficult, if not impossible. In addition, those who appear on sex offender registries are specifically registered because they have already been formally punished. Do registries perform only a managerial function, or do they continue the punishment that, for other types of offenders, would largely be concluded upon release (or would be "more concluded" upon release)?

Not all sexual assaults are reported, nor are all offenders convicted. But those who are identified generate an ire reserved wholly for them. Sexual offenders elicit a fear and revulsion unparalleled by other types of offenders and, if incarcerated, may be victims of "prison justice" themselves. The reasons for the animosity toward sex offenders are many, but figuring most significantly is the public perception that sex offenders are highly likely to reoffend and, therefore, require distinctive means by which they are to be dealt with, often in the name of public security.

In his examination of crime and punishment, Garland (1990) suggests that criminology is not simply a discipline but may also be seen as a cultural discourse, with criminological concepts often being taken up by society as a means of understanding difficult social phenomenon. As Bill Hebenton and Terry Thomas (1996) explain, "The special nature of sexual offending and more importantly the problems of *reoffending* (*recidivism*) and '*treatment*' act as crucial reference points in understanding public perception" (430). Yet while these concepts are often referred to by both the public and criminologists, Hebenton and Thomas observe that there is, in fact, little in the way of "settled ground" among academics with respect to the likelihood of reoffending or the successes of treatment. Related to the problem of estimating reoffending is the problem of offense specialization: not all sexual offenders commit similar crimes thereafter. Similarly, those who have committed other nonsexual offenses may commit sexual offenses in the future. Past behavior does not represent a dependable trajectory upon which expectations of the future can be built.

However, the past, unlike the future, is knowable, and as our discussion of risk suggests, information that we are able to collect on past behavior provides guidance for assessing the probability that similar actions will occur in the future. We know that some convicted sex offenders have committed further crimes upon their release, and we know that the consequences of these crimes have been grave. This is coupled with the fact that social ties have tended to erode with modernization, and levels of personal anxiety are on the increase. The message that the public is increasingly given is that safety and security is a personal endeavor—the police cannot be expected to shoulder alone the burden of public security. "Social order is increasingly thought of as something which cannot merely be protected and maintained but which must, rather, be actively constructed and managed if the social and personal costs of insecurity are to be minimized" (Hebenton and Thomas 1996, 431). The way in which security is actively constructed is by acquiring knowledge of the hazards and opportunities in our respective environments in order to be able to safely navigate our daily lives. The police (and to a lesser extent, other social control agencies) become responsible for the distribution of information or knowledge that will enable individuals to assess and manage the hazards they may face: knowledge enables risk assessment and risk management.

One means of providing knowledge about the hazards in one's environment is through the development of a sex offender registry. Abril Bedarf explains that registries generally consist of four different types:

1. the public may access information directly from the police, which entails going to the police station and looking at pictures of released sex offenders;
2. the public may call a "900" number to find out if a particular individual resides at a specific address;
3. there is a mandatory self-registry or self-identification to the police; and
4. there is discretionary or mandatory police identification (in Hebenton and Thomas 1996, 438).

We consider sex offender registries first in terms of their impact on public security and, second, with respect to their impact on offenders' rights.

In perhaps one of the most famous cases, and certainly one of the cases that has been the driver behind public concern and subsequent U.S. legislation with respect to sex offender registries, was the death of Megan Kanka, a seven-year-old who was raped and killed by a known sexual offender. In the aftermath of the crime, Megan's parents emphatically stated that, had they known a convicted sexual offender lived in their community, they would never have let Megan travel so freely about her neighborhood. The parents' claim was that they would have taken different (and protective) action had they known this hazard existed in such close proximity to their family. Not unlike other families, the Kankas would have assessed their risk of harm differently and adjusted their actions accordingly. Without knowing this hazard/offender existed, they were not able to accurately assess their environment and therefore were at a huge disadvantage that ultimately cost them dearly.

As a means of establishing security, it is necessary to be able to identify where potential hazards lie in order to manage the risk of harm. Basically, in order to establish security, vulnerabilities must first be identified. The police participate in this risk assessment by identifying harms and potential harms. But both the police and the public operate in contexts of limited resources to deal with identified harms. As the police role has continued to expand over the years, the ability to address crime prevention and to effectively respond to crime is restricted by the realities of limited resources to deal with "what is," versus "what may be": "what may be" brings us into the realm of possibility only. Part of the task of managing an expanding realm of hazards involves the devolution of responsibility away from the police, with the police acting more particularly as knowledge brokers (see, again, Ericson and Haggerty 1997). Rather than, for example, parking a police car in front of a potential offender's house, the responsibility for addressing an identified threat has been turned over to the public or neighborhood themselves. The police provide the public with information. Citizens, in turn, must determine the most appropriate course of action given their resources. Responsibility for action is therefore increasingly that of the public, not the police agency.

In terms of what they refer to as the "political economy of risk," Hebenton and Thomas suggest that the mobilization of particular groups, such as communities, to address identified harms is a cost-effective measure for the police. Legislation may be created that facilitates the release of information, effectively removing some responsibility from the police, while placing more responsibility on the shoulders of the public. The release of information is facilitated, at least in part, by legislation that enables access to information; at the same time, this legislation may trade police responsibility for public responsibility. In order that responsibility for security is taken up by the public, the public must first be made aware of its vulnerability by exposing the threats (providing information) that exist around it.

The impact of knowing the identities and whereabouts of known offenders, however, has an impact on overall security that is not entirely productive and may not lead to an overall increase in security. First, while the identification of a specific threat may lead the public to adapt to, and possibly change, its behavior with respect to that specific threat, there may be a host of other threats that are equally endangering but are not as yet formally identified. For example, not every new sexual offense is committed by an individual involved in a past sexual offense. As we note above, the patterns with respect to offending are not clear; therefore, keeping track of a known offender in no way reduces the overall pool from which subsequent offenders might be drawn. Those who have previously committed thefts or minor assaults—or have not committed any previous crimes—might commit sexual offenses in the future. Associated with this point is that sex offender registries appear to assume that sex offenders are predators only outside of their doorsteps—that they are somehow incapable of targeting victims outside their immediate vicinity (a point we made earlier about the risk to victims from those who live with them).

Second, even if subsequent sex offenses are committed by those who have done so in the past, very few of their previous offenses ever come to the attention of the authorities. Those sex offenders who are identified on sex offender registries are likely a very select sample of offenders who happen to have been caught (either, perhaps, through effective police investigations or through their own stupidity).

Third, the provision of information about offenders such as found in sex offender registries appears to make the tacit assumption that, once communities know of the hazards in their environment, they will also have the resources to protect themselves from these hazards. Yet, individuals and families must make choices with respect to limited resources; some options, such as moving, may simply be out of the range of possibility.

The idea of sex offender registries and pinpointing specific individuals as threats to particular segments of the population is problematic on a number of levels. When identifying at-risk individuals, those who are more likely to either offend or be victimized than the rest of the population, there are a host of other variables that must also come into play in order to produce a certain outcome, whether that outcome is desired or not. We know, for example, that not every ADHD (attention deficit/hyperactivity disorder) eight-year-old child is a future criminal, just as not every rule-abiding sixteen-year-old will necessarily avoid crime in the future. The past does not predetermine the future. Further, the sex offender registry may inhibit the individual from ever making a productive contribution to society because of being labeled as a perpetual threat. As Richard

Tewksbury and Elizabeth Mustaine (2006) observe, however, "Most public and political concerns center on control rather than facilitating re-entry and reintegration" (62). Risk management issues therefore take center stage at the expense of the specific individuals involved. Sex offender registrants illustrate the intersection of risk and security in specific and public ways.

One of the difficulties associated with assessing individual risk is the recognition that there are no guarantees regarding future behavior. In order to address this uncertainty, the tendency in law has been to err on the side of caution. While the probability of reoffending is not known, the fact that previous sex offenders have committed further similar crimes upon their release has encouraged legislators to take a dim view of the future behavior of released sex offenders. The case of a failed challenge to Alaska's sex offender registry and community notification begins with the following: "Sex offenders exact a uniquely severe and unremitting toll on the Nation and its citizens for three basic reasons: 'they are the least likely to be cured'; 'they are the most likely to reoffend'; and 'they prey on the most innocent members of our society.'"[3] According to law (and public perception), there is no such thing as "no risk" when it comes to sex offenders—they therefore have to be managed accordingly. This management comes in the form of postrelease supervision, in this case, by way of sex offender registration and community notification. At the same time, while the police hold information with respect to who is registered, the specific supervision of released offenders does not typically figure into the supervisory duties of the police themselves. The institutional management of the offender has been pushed onto the public.

What does this mean for the offender? Sex offender registries "can be seen as reifying the 'permanence' and 'prevalence' of risk attached to sexual offenders" (Hebenton and Thomas 1996, 436)—independent of any further signs of offending on the part of identified individuals. The actuarial premises of sex offender registries are clear: persons who have committed certain types of crime are placed into a particular risk category, independent of their specific circumstances or the characteristics of the communities in which they plan to reside. Legal challenges to the ex post facto arguments have failed, with such challenges being met with responses such as the following:

> Registration and notification provisions are a reasonable means of promoting public safety because they reduce the vulnerability of potential victims and deny prospective offenders the anonymity and secrecy on which they so heavily depend. The law provides citizens with information concerning the existence and offense patterns of offenders living, working, or studying near them. With such information in hand, *individuals can protect themselves and their children by increasing their alertness and modifying their conduct in a manner that minimizes their risk of falling victim to a crime.* (italics added)[4]

The argument goes on to state,

> In any event, *given the recidivist tendencies of sex offenders as a class, singling out those individual offenders who might pose a diminished risk of reoffending is an inordinately difficult and error-prone task, in an area where the costs of a mistaken judgment can be devastating.* Alaska thus reasonably chose to allow members of the public to make those risk determinations themselves. (italics added)[5]

Individual differences are considered unimportant—membership in a class of offenders usurps any consideration of individual situations.

The imposition on the lives of individuals who have served their sentence is justified based on risk-based understandings of security. As noted above, the costs of reoffending are seen as simply too great to take the chance that offenders will not reoffend. Further, particular offenders, by the nature of the crimes they commit, essentially remove themselves from the constitutional protections that may be afforded others who commit various crimes: "Persons found to have committed a sex offense have a reduced expectation of privacy because of the public's interest in public safety" (Washington Law 1990, ch. 3, 116, in Hebenton and Thomas 1996, 439).

Alternatively, how effective is targeted intervention with regard to specific individuals? Targeted intervention involves the identification of a particular threat or offender, with specific measures taken against that offender to reduce, if not remove, the threat that he or she poses to a specific victim.

Dealing with Hazards in the Aftermath: Offenders

One particular method of attempting to control the future threat that an offender poses is to punish. As suggested earlier, punishments may be considered consequentialist or nonconsequentialist. In an early critique of selective incapacitation, a consequentialist approach, Andrew von Hirsch (1984) explains that a central difficulty with predictive sentencing is that it falsely predicts: many schemes overpredict in that they predict that certain offenders will offend in the future who never actually do offend. Von Hirsch explains that using such schemes is particularly problematic: "Punishment, as a blaming institution, is warranted only for past culpable choices and cannot be justly levied for future criminal conduct. Unless the person actually makes the predicted choice, he cannot be blamed for it" (178). Von Hirsch further explains that selective incapacitation tends to give greater weight to aspects of an offender's record having little to do with blameworthiness. For example, rather than weighing past convictions more heavily, selective incapacitation may instead focus on criminal activity in general—not simply crimes for which convictions have been dealt. In addition, offenders who have committed similar crimes in the past may be punished more harshly than those who commit new types of crime.

The idea of attempting to know the future through patterns of offending has been taken up by researchers who consider various life-course perspectives. Robert Sampson and John Laub (1993) suggest there are various transitions and turning points that lead individuals to change their offending behaviors. Marriage, for example, can lead to changes in both frequencies of criminal opportunities as well as the types of criminal opportunities (McGloin et al. 2007). Specialization among offenders may be the result of having fewer contacts and in turn fewer opportunities to offend. For example, self-control, for propensity theorists, is thought not to be influenced by life events such as marriage, primarily because those with criminal propensities will tend not to experience these events in the first place (those with low self-control are less likely to be married). Further, those characterized by "variations in criminal propensity also influence whether one perceives the existence of criminal opportunities in any given situation" (McGloin et al. 2007, 326).

In their study of convicted felons and consideration of their life courses, and specifically their "street time"—time out of prison over the course of a two-year period—McGloin and her colleagues found the following: "Within-individual changes in community supervision, marriage, and drug and alcohol use are related to the level of offending diversity" (335). This suggests that short-term changes to an individual's life will produce changes—for better or for worse—in his or her likelihood of offending due to changes in opportunities. At the same time, these authors found that indicators of propensity continue to play a key role: "Findings support the general notion that the more highly motivated crime-prone offenders are more likely to engage in a wide range of criminal behaviors relative to their less motivated, more criminally specialized, counterparts" (McGloin et al. 2007, 337). What this means for individual offenders is that they may alter their short-term offending at particular life points and become more specialized, but as the time window under consideration increases, versatility also increases. These authors make the point that considerations of future offending must include both motivational and situational considerations.

DOMESTIC VIOLENCE (SPECIFIC/INDIVIDUAL)

As with states and institutions, an individual must also respond to the fact that he or she has been the victim of a particular crime. What does it mean to individuals when they experience a crime? How do they register this event in the broader scheme of experience? There are many factors that impact how individuals perceive and deal with their own victimization. First, the nature of the crime is important. The theft of one's backpack, for example, impacts an individual much differently than a personal assault. A victimization that includes hospitalization is likely to be perceived differently than a victimization that is an inconvenience.

Second, the context of the crime also determines how one registers the impact of victimization. Contexts include many factors: the relationship of the offender to the victim, the time of day, and the geographic location, for instance. Personal qualities and characteristics also clearly impact how individuals perceive victimization: those with greater self-confidence, for example, attribute responsibility for crimes differently than those who are less self-confident. Similarly, those who are younger reflect on victimization differently than those who are older; and men consider victimization differently than women. Related to how individuals reconcile their victimization is the fit (or lack thereof) with behaviors they have experienced or witnessed in the past. Being a witness to violence while growing up, for example, makes the violence that one experiences later in life less consequential than among those without such previous life experiences. Finally, the manner in which others respond to victimization will have consequences for how individuals come to define and address their victimization experiences. Support or lack thereof from friends and family will influence how victimization is perceived. Formal recognition of experiences as "crime," either by the application of formal charges by police or informal acknowledgment by friends, family, welfare, or other agencies also impacts how individuals interpret their experiences.

To a large degree, victimization is not limited to those who directly experience it. As Uwe Ewald points out, and as we suggested above, crime is a cultural discourse and serves as a metaphor of threat even for those who have not experienced it. The *idea* of crime is threatening even if we have never directly experienced crime, thus creating feelings of being at risk and perpetuating feelings of general insecurity (Ewald 2000, 176). But the likelihood of victimization is not as all-pervasive as this discourse suggests. Those who are most likely to offend are also most likely to be victimized. This means that, rather than individual propensities toward crime (and victimization), there may be categorical disadvantages that characterize certain groups of people. At the same time, the rhetoric associated with the idea of crime is that we must take individual responsibility for our own safety. Those who do not avoid victimization therefore may be considered blameworthy in that they have failed to adequately protect themselves. Avoiding victimization becomes an issue for the "individual management of risk" (Stanko 2000, 26), rather than a problem of collective disadvantage. Elizabeth Stanko observes, "As the debate turns to discussions of risk avoidance, and especially that avoidance which can be orchestrated by individuals themselves, there is a failure to engage with the wider debate about unsafety arising from structural disadvantage" (27).

Feminist scholarship has emphasized that, far from being a haven of safety and security, home can be a place of violence and fear. For women, the likelihood of becoming a victim is far greater in the home than on the streets. The rhetoric of the "safe home" perpetuates the idea that the streets, and the stranger, are more dangerous than the home and the threats posed by intimates found therein. Advice with respect to personal crime prevention has tended to focus on public spaces, ignoring the fact that private space is where women (and some men) experience greater levels of violence from intimates. Protection against those within the home does not fall into the realm of typical "safety talk" (Corteen 2002).

At least part of the difficulty in dealing with domestic violence emanates from the association of "domestic" with "home" and with "private": domestic (interfamilial) practices undertaken within the home have been considered private. The association of the term "domestic" with both "private" and "home" confuses responses to violence between intimates. Interpersonal (domestic) relationships and practices are not private when one party is in danger, nor are homes necessarily the site of comfort and security. A further challenge associated with domestic violence is that the violence persists—targets of domestic violence are often subject to repeated incidents of abuse.

The majority of victims of domestic violence are women. While the range of types of women and men involved in domestic violence is wide, the issue of control figures centrally in this behavior, with one or the other partner attempting to exert control. The characteristic of control is not exclusive to domestic violence situations as compared to other violent encounters, but an additional characteristic, that of entrapment, may be accentuated in these situations. Entrapment may be economic, social, or emotional but may also be the result of fear for one's own or one's children's safety. Angelo Moe (2007) explains that women become entrapped due to control tactics by abusers, as well as the failure of social institutions to adequately address the circumstances of abused women.

Official responses to situations of domestic violence by police have been varied, with an initial hesitation to consider these situations as criminal due, in part, to the conflation of domestic with private. In recent years, however, as we discussed in chapter 2, mandatory arrest or preferred arrest policies have been implemented, meaning that action is backed by policies that require particular responses. Efforts that move beyond the police have involved other social agencies in "coordinated community responses" (CCR). CCR involves, as Jeffrey Bouffard and Lisa Muftic (2007) explain, "(1) improved system effectiveness; (2) delineation of services across agencies; (3) delivery of appropriate services to the victim with minimal distress; (4) protection of the victim; and (5) successful sanctioning of the offender" (354).

The question that burns in the minds of those who are not involved in domestic violence situations is why don't these people get out? Self-preservation, in terms of increased likelihood of violence during separation, is part of this answer. As Kristin Anderson (2007) further explains, drawing on the work of Goetting (1999), "Leaving is a process rather than a one-time event . . . internal and external changes can serve as catalysts for getting out" (177). Internal changes include shifts in assessing blame and guilt, while external changes include changing structural opportunities, such as shifts in social networks and social services. The aftermath for victims who are able to identify a specific threat in their lives is clearly fraught with ambiguity and lack of resources both at the personal and structural levels.

As mentioned earlier, the source of threat or harm impacts the nature of the victim's (and outsiders') response to victimization. The efforts of victims of domestic violence to address their situations have been met in the past with reactions from observers who fail to legitimate these experiences as "real" victimization. Victim satisfaction with police services is notably higher when victimization involves a stranger relationship (see, for example, Byrne, Kilpatrick, and Howley 1999; Felson and Pare 2007). There are other situations, however, where the responsibility for harm is clearly attributable to an identifiable source and when victims are seen as deserving compensation for their losses. Compensation does not reduce the probability of similar events in the future but is typically meant to reestablish a playing field that more closely approximates the original—previctimization—state of affairs.

Compensation is defined as the provision of financial or other resources that are used to reimburse, balance, or pay back the costs or losses associated with a particular event. In terms of crime, the idea of compensation has been most closely associated with restorative justice and the notion that the offender must "make good" with the victim, especially in terms of redressing monetary losses. Compensation between victims and offenders outside of restorative justice contexts is relatively rare, as the system of justice more common throughout the Western world focuses more specifically on retribution by the state against the offender, removing victims from the equation. Yet, compensation schemes between government and individual victims are somewhat more common, with one such example including the September 11 Victim Compensation Fund.

Edward Lascher and Michael Powers (2004) provide a number of principles suggesting criteria for when compensation by government should be provided. While their analysis was directed toward terrorism and other disasters, their work also provides insight into the realm of compensation for crime. First, Lascher and Powers suggest, "it seems natural to argue that government should compensate victims if government could have done more to avoid/mitigate losses but failed to do so (or if indeed government were directly responsible for exposing individuals to risk, as in a mandatory inoculation program)" (287). One might therefore imagine contexts where police have failed to protect citizens through some type of abrogation of duty. We know of one such case involving Jane Doe, who sued the Metropolitan Toronto Police Service for failing to provide public warnings regarding a known (rapist) hazard, arguing that this failure resulted in Doe's subsequent rape (Van Brunschot and Kennedy 2004).

Second, Lascher and Powers argue that government compensation could be reduced somewhat if victims failed to take certain reasonable pre-event measures in the face of risk, yet the government shoulders more responsibility for compensation because it is expected to have greater access to risk assessment indicators than will particular individuals. In other words, not everyone has the same access to information, and those with greater access bear more responsibility than those with less access. Third, government should compensate when failing to do so puts individuals at increased risk of subsequent harm.

SUMMING UP

This chapter has focused on the aftermath of crime and how risk plays into our responses to it. We reviewed how crime data have been used and the ways in which crime trends have been interpreted, highlighting the difficulties with predictions of future crime levels based on what has happened in the past. Quetelet's observations from over a century ago highlight why the notion of "average man" is problematic as it relates to specific individuals and yet can be surprisingly accurate when it comes to describing what various populations or subpopulations might do in the future.

Our discussion of hate crime and sex offender registries expanded more specifically on categories of crimes and the difficulties such categories pose for understanding these crimes and for determining appropriate responses both formally and informally to certain types of crimes, as well as the difficulties that prevail for individuals who are defined as being particular types of offenders. Individuals who are in the position of offender or victim may find that their situations are compromised after crimes have taken place. Some offenders, for example, are dealt with in ways that overstate the particular danger they pose to the public despite having served time for their crimes. Similarly, the means by which particular victims are dealt with may be obstructed by virtue of their membership in specific categories—categorizations that are built on historical circumstances having little to do with them—yet similarly constrain the ways they are treated by both the public and the criminal justice system.

We make the point that our responses to crime are often oriented to redressing the past or addressing the future. When we attempt to redress harm, we orient ourselves specifically to the past and the harm that has been done—redressing harm is backward looking. On the other hand, we may orient our responses with a view to the future and base our responses to a particular crime or criminal with an expectation of what we want the future to hold—a forward-looking approach. This is the idea behind deterrence—we may deliver (or threaten to deliver) punishments to crime with an eye to creating a specific future. Both approaches have difficulties associated with them, and neither has any guarantees.

Risk plays specifically into the aftermath of crime by orienting us to the future—in many cases, the goal is to prevent the recurrence of crime and to learn from the past. If we choose to punish the harm done by a crime, we either compromise or positively impact the future and create a different likelihood of crime than previously existed. For example, the offender who feels he was harshly punished may feel little regard for the society that punished him in the first instance, thereby increasing the likelihood that he will reoffend. On the other hand, we could respond to crimes by creating a specific future that enables offenders to reintegrate into society and reduce the likelihood of future criminal activity. Yet, there is no guarantee that the risk of crime will be reduced in either approach. Clearly, responding to crime in ways that will minimize the likelihood of future involvement in crime represents a quagmire of issues and potential difficulties.

Throughout this chapter, we have suggested there are problems in relying too closely on the past as a means to predict the future. Undoubtedly, however, the present and future may depend heavily on what has already transpired. The aftermath of every situation is clearly the beginning of the next potential crime—the challenge is to learn from the past yet not be bound to it.

REVISITING THE RISK IN CRIME MATRIX

In the last three chapters, we have provided examples of crime concepts that illustrate our crime matrix. We've focused on threats that occur, first, in temporally distinct phases of crime events—in the precursor, transaction, and aftermath phases. Second, we've highlighted threats that are abstract or those that are more concrete. Finally, we've suggested that threats are directed toward, or impact, specific levels of analysis, from individuals, to institutions, to states. By highlighting how these three dimensions (time, nature of threat, and level of analysis) intersect, we demonstrate how the concept of risk is central to our understandings and explanations of crime threats and realities. The concept of risk, we argue, underpins all crime study—in attempting to predict, explain, or assess crime, the underlying goal is typically to reduce the probability of crime occurring or reoccurring.

The very basis of risk or probability theory is that some event will happen—something always happens. The efforts of police and theorists are often an attempt to reduce the probability that something bad (criminal) will occur, at the same time increasing the probability that something positive will occur. Unfortunately, efforts to increase the likelihood of positive over negative outcomes are not always successful. One of the most significant impacts on our ability to reduce the probability of crime is the quality of the information we have at hand. This is an issue that is central to all dimensions of our crime matrix: we can only plan to address negative outcomes if, first, we imagine the possibility of a threat occurring (obviously more a problem in the case of abstract threats), and second, we have accurate information about the threat, including information that is both complete and correct.

In our earlier discussions, we considered the impact of perception and politics in our understandings of what constitutes endangerment or threat—whether at the individual, institutional, or state levels. We noted that perceptions may not be accurate; the work of Kahneman and Tversky, for example, suggests that at the same time that perceptions facilitate understanding, in other cases, perceptions get in the way of assessing our environments accurately. Perceptions not only impact our interpretations of the information we have but also limit our ability to seek more or different information. We also suggested that the risk of crime is managed by political factors that have little to do with the reality of crime risk. We observed that crime rates, for example, are a product of policing initiatives and mandates and cannot be considered a complete measure of how much crime is out there. While it may be difficult, if not impossible, to remove the impact of perceptions and politics from how crime risk is viewed, the goal is, rather, to develop awareness of these factors as limitations and as something to consider in terms of how we understand and respond to crime risk.

Beyond perceptions and politics, there are other factors that limit our ability to wrestle with crime risk. In particular, we tend to prioritize what we can measure over what is meaningful, especially with respect to forming actuarially based understandings of where crime risk lays. Profiling is a prime example. It is true that we can measure demographic characteristics such as age, income, education, criminal record, and so forth, but the categories we create from this knowledge do not provide us with the insight we need with regard to predicting who will offend. We do not necessarily have information on the types of factors that are equally important in predicting whether or not an individual commits a future crime—relationships with peers, with family, and so on, and other factors that are critical to predicting likelihood of future offending. Earlier, we mentioned efforts to identify high-risk offenders—each of whom has particular characteristics that inspire observers to stereotype (or profile) according to the characteristics of these offenders. The media also play a role in creating stereotyped profiles of offenders by reporting on certain types of crimes committed by certain groups to the exclusion of other crime threats. A recent spate of gang-related killings in Alberta, for example, may cause audiences of media reports to assume that the greatest crime risk they face is that by gangs. However, it is worth noting that one has a far greater chance of being robbed or assaulted at home than being caught in the cross fire of a gang shooting.

The information that is used in the determination of crime risk is therefore less than perfect. Trial and error play a role in how crime risk may be assessed, but the difficulty, of course, with this risk assessment strategy alone is that this type of learning comes in the aftermath—after a crime has been committed. At the same time, the aftermath of every crime event is the precursor stage to the next, so it could be expected that assessments of the probability of crime, and how it can be prevented, will change over time. We distinguish between abstract and specific threats, with the type of threat playing a significant role in what can be done to prepare for (the precursor stage), experience (transaction phase), and address (aftermath) various types of threats. Terrorism is a good example of an abstract threat—our success at meeting the challenges of this threat will only be known in the context of the occurrence of a specific terrorist event. If a terrorist event occurs, one might be able to guess that preparations for this (previously abstract and now concrete) threat failed (or succeeded in terms of damage control, for example). On the other hand, the absence of a specific terrorist event cannot necessarily be attributed to any of the efforts that were made to prevent it from occurring. An abstract threat that does not materialize cannot be said to have been prevented—it just didn't occur. While some agencies may find it tempting to take credit for nonevents, because the probability of the event occurring in the first place was unknown, the absence of the event does not mean that prevention efforts were successful.

There is, then, a greater degree of difficulty associated with risk assessment when it comes to abstract threats, precisely because there is often little information that can be used to establish the probabilities of particular events. Terrorist events, for example, are no doubt low probability, but they are also high damage when they do occur, making them particularly problematic. With more abstract threats, the information that is needed to determine probabilities is often sketchy or nonexistent and fails to reach the level necessary to realize the potential of prevention efforts. Unfortunately, even when dealing with specific threats, we may not have the right information at hand to determine whether our prevention efforts are effective and whether we are appropriately managing risk.

NOTES

1. As we discussed above, we recognize the difficulties associated with relying too heavily on crime rates as the definitive picture of crime, but crime rates fit well with the concept of risk, as the appearance of patterns, or lack thereof, are often used to portend the future.

2. Having said this, we recognize that in contexts of fear certain discriminatory practices are indeed relied upon, though framed in ways that suggest that these practices are for the greater good. For example, we see the detainment of various individuals under the auspices of the USA Patriot Act. This act operates under the assumption that the damage a terrorist could inflict is much greater than the damage that might be done if a suspect's rights are violated.

3. *Godfrey and Botelho v. John Doe I et al.*, No. 01-729, 2.

4. *Godfrey and Botelho v. John Doe I et al.*, 11, 30.

5. *Godfrey and Botelho v. John Doe I et al.*, 12.

5

Integrating Risk

At the beginning of our discussion of risk, in chapter 1, we presented a risk matrix that considered three key dimensions of our understanding of risk (see table 1.1). First, there is the nature of the threat under examination—is the threat known and specific, or is it uncertain and abstract? The specific or general nature of the threats and hazards considered are critical to determining how we might address future probabilities. A second key dimension is that of time. The previous chapters suggested that there is a time element to risk: there is the anticipatory or precursor phase. Threats and opportunities present themselves, yet in the anticipatory phase, little harm has yet been done. There is a transaction phase—the threat has been actualized or the hazard has caused damage. Finally, there is a postevent or aftermath phase, where incidents have occurred and responses are underway. This phase also constitutes the anticipatory phase for future (similar) events.

A third dimension that we have taken into account is level of analysis, including whether we are considering individuals, institutions, or states. Level of analysis, however, is really a shortcut term to refer to a number of considerations. We must consider, first, against whom or what are threats directed: toward an individual or an agency? Who, in other words, is the expected victim? Second, we must consider by whom or from what the threat is emanating. Is the source of threat an individual, a group, or a state? The way in which we address threat will be determined at least in part by its source. Finally, level of analysis also relates to responsibility for dealing with and managing hazards. It seems relatively clear, for example, that states will likely be in the best position to deal with threats that come from other states. On the other hand, it may be less clear who or what is responsible for dealing with the case of crime threats that come from individuals targeting other individuals. While the criminal justice system (including police and the courts) assumes the role of and acts for the victim in court proceedings, only a portion of incidents come to the attention of police (as suggested by victimization surveys), and even fewer still come through the courts. As we have suggested earlier, many threats and hazards are simply dealt with informally, independent of any official determination of wrongdoing.

In the previous chapters, we considered level of analysis primarily in terms of the targets of threat, or against whom crime threats have been directed, though in some cases we considered the source of threat as well. To carry this analysis forward, we need to highlight and reflect on level of analysis in terms of *responsibility* for dealing with threat. In particular, we note that different agencies focus on different elements of crime risk, according to the nature of the threats under consideration, as well as the temporal phase and resources available to particular agencies. Specifically, we consider an integrated model, parts of which highlight approaches taken by particular agencies or by particular perspectives. We again note that these approaches address time, as well as type of threat.

INTEGRATING APPROACHES TO RISK IN CRIME

Our discussion to this point highlights the observation that, rather than distinct explanations of crime, or distinct ways of addressing crime, many seemingly disparate approaches to crime concepts are increasingly compatible when one considers these approaches as housed within an overarching crime risk matrix. This matrix makes compatibility more obvious by emphasizing how it is that particular concepts address different aspects of the risk enterprise: some focus on precursors of crime and so may be located in the anticipatory phase of our framework. We see references to those who might be at risk due to certain characteristics or experiences that might predispose them to particular behaviors. Other concepts focus on the deterrent aspects of punishment and how specific formal or informal responses may increase or decrease the likelihood of future crime. Still other theories focus on how it is that we interact in situations of immediate crime hazard—for most of us, we respond in ways that we expect will minimize our losses, and maximize our gains, regardless of whether we are victims or offenders.

Similarly, agencies charged with the task of assessing and managing crime threat may be geared toward different types of threat and have different resources at their disposal. The police, for instance, may see themselves as serving anticipatory functions—attempting to prevent crime before it happens; transaction functions, such as minimizing damage during crime transactions (if they happen to arrive while crimes are in progress, for example); and recovery functions, which entail investigation of crimes after they occur. Further, the police deal with threats that come from various sources, though they tend to focus on individual-level sources of threat to the relative exclusion of crimes perpetrated by agencies (such as occur in terms of white-collar crime, etc.).

This is the point at which we are asked whether we are trying to build a new theory to supplant the ones that already exist. Does the risk approach simply become an alternative to social disorganization theory or social control theory? Our task is to move our thinking to a level that takes into account risk approaches across many crime concepts and theories. But, as we have shown in our discussion in previous chapters, this approach is more integrative with than in opposition to other perspectives. The framework we offer in table 5.1 suggests how this integration can take place, redefining the cells at each level to characterize how risk is manifest at each stage.

The advantage of the approach suggested by this model is that it illustrates potential combinations of different strategies depending on proximity to and nature of threats. It captures risk as a dynamic process, which can range from uncertainty to more specific guidelines for response. It also accounts for important interaction effects (between time and nature of threats), with the addition of ideas like vulnerability and exposure. Where the event perspectives (Sacco and Kennedy 2002; Meier, Kennedy, and Sacco 2001; Agnew 2006) have shown that we can account for different theoretical approaches depending on the temporal aspect of the event we are studying, this analysis takes us to the next level, adding an anticipatory element to our analysis through the identification of concepts and theoretical orientations that may coincide with different elements of the dimensions under consideration. We are able, then, to take into account uncertainty and how this can be dealt with through surveillance, for example, but also how specific threats may be managed through a strategy such as situational prevention. We can situate the vulnerability and exposure that comes from the presence of motivated offenders but also from the threats posed by social disorganization.

Table 5.1. Mapping Risk

	→ Time →		
Type of Threat	*Precursor*	*Transaction*	*Aftermath*
Abstract	Uncertainty	Exposure	Prevention/Preparedness
⇡⇣	Threat	Vulnerability	Consequence
Specific	Hazard	Incident	Recovery

The framework provides a way of moving from the point of risk assessment, through to risk management and risk governance. Instead of having a patchwork of theories that are set up to compete against one another, this approach brings these ideas more closely together. The goal, then, is to identify and articulate (assess) the elements that increase the probability of crime to develop strategies to manage and reduce this likelihood. To show how this can be done, we offer a risk model that includes a case study that brings together the important elements we have discussed. In this discussion, we use the case study to explain what is meant by uncertainty, exposure, and vulnerability. We will also illustrate how these concepts are connected to threats and hazards and examine how these can lead to strategies related to prevention and response.

INTRODUCING THE ACTION MODEL

To this point, we have provided a review of how risk is considered through the eyes of criminologists and criminal justice experts who apply this concept (often indirectly) in theory building and research. This work provides an important matrix for our rethinking some of the basic premises of crime analysis. It includes a more proactive and less reactive perspective. It emphasizes the importance of accounting for uncertainty and considering crime events in the context of probabilistic outcomes. It also encourages risk assessment procedures that coordinate the activities of all parties in the crime-prevention and response community. But the transition from the theoretical ideas presented earlier to the more programmatic approaches required in implementing risk assessments demand that we reconsider our matrix and adapt it to a new purpose and different audience: law enforcement.

We had an ideal opportunity to make sense of this transition when we were involved in a session of police leaders held at the Turkish International Academy against Drugs and Organized Crime (TADOC) training center on drug enforcement and organized crime in Ankara, Turkey. This center provides instruction for officers in the Turkish National Police but also brings in police leaders from many other countries. Offered the opportunity to work with them on developing a training program on risk assessment, we confronted the challenge of explaining the risk ideas presented in the previous chapters in a way that would make sense in day-to-day operations headed up by the participants in our course. To begin, we asked each participant in the session to explain how he used risk assessment in his work, which involved everything from tracking drug smugglers to tackling minor street crime. All of the officers indicated that they assessed risk every day; they just didn't call it that. In addition, when asked what concepts they might apply in developing their assessments, they were unable to articulate anything in particular. As we have explained, they understood that assessing the likelihood of criminal activity or harm was a central part of everything they did: the officers' own likelihood of harm, the public's risk of victimization, and offenders' likelihood of criminal activity—this was always dealt with as background context but rarely explicitly articulated or built into programs or plans.

The police leadership in Turkey is uniformly well educated and has been exposed to a variety of modern police tactics, so their responses did not come from a lack of familiarity with crime theories and prevention strategies. It appeared mostly to come from the fact that little had been done to expose them to these ideas—in a way not at all dissimilar to the experience in North American policing. At the same time, abstract risk concepts that they did know about were not easy to apply to their circumstances. They felt that the ideas were too general or not pertinent to their tactical plans. Yet, they were open to frameworks that would provide a means by which they could become more proactive, taking on risk assessment as a way of redirecting their efforts and justifying their actions.

It became apparent in our discussions with these officers that we needed to take our risk matrix and rework it for use in practical policing terms. In a repackaged format, we developed a framework that includes assessment, accountability, and governance issues that provide clear guidelines in applying risk concepts to operational policing issues. We used the ideas laid out in table 5.1 and then adapted them to fit the practical needs of policing. As is often the case in developing these kinds of frameworks, the task is made easier if we are able to summarize the elements in a simple statement or in an easy to remember acronym. We came up with the idea of a framework referred to as the ACTION model, with the word itself providing an impetus for police leaders to see themselves as proactive in addition to actively seeking out risk-based solutions to their problems. The ideas represented by each letter are explained in table 5.2.

Table 5.2.   The ACTION Model

ACTION—Risk Model

*A*ssessing Uncertainties, Threats, and Hazards (Risk Assessment)
Making *C*onnections
Setting *T*asks to Respond and Prevent (Risk Management)
Collecting *I*nformation about the Event
Refining the *O*rganization (Risk Governance)
*N*otifying Others

This approach incorporates the three elements that are important for risk evaluation: risk assessment, risk management, and risk governance. These articulate the application of the different aspects of the risk model (table 5.1) in a way that provides practical guidelines to practitioners applying a risk approach to their work. Once again, the risk approach provides a flexible way for us to repackage ideas and make them work in a way that directs action and assesses the value of the interventions that are planned. The risk model promotes, as we have said, a forward-looking approach and provides parameters for evaluation and ways to improve the job that is done in responding to crime problems. Underlying these elements is the basic view that the agency engaged in this incorporates risk-based intelligence through means that promote proactive rather than reactive planning. We are interested in the extent to which these elements are found in agencies and the degree to which the different parts of organizations use this method to guide their operations.

A CASE STUDY

In our experience with the Turkish police, we found that they were able to use the ACTION model to address specific crime problems and sort out the steps they needed to follow to conduct strategic risk planning. To illustrate how this can be done, we will use an example from the experience with crime in a North American city to show how this model provides guidelines to incorporate risk planning into police decision making.

> The case involves a highly disorganized community in which there has been a serious problem with interpersonal violence, in particular, shootings, set into the context of widespread drug dealing (apparently operated under the auspices of competing gangs, the members of which live throughout the community). The local police have been unable to deal with either the drug problem or the violence problem and are restricted to post duties and traffic enforcement. The heavy lifting in enforcement is delivered by a special force of state and federal agents assigned to the community, but their numbers are limited (constituting about a quarter of the municipal force), and while they have had success in increasing the clearance rates on shootings (rising from about 10 percent to about 40 percent in two years), the task of managing this area is still daunting, particularly as the onerous aspects of processing arrests have made these police agencies less efficient in pursuing crime. The police leadership is concerned that the drug problem is not abating, and violence, while suppressed, is likely to spike up again without a sustained attack on the basic factors driving the crime patterns.

In addressing this case study, we can use the ACTION model to sort out the various aspects of risk and tie them to organizational responses that are appropriate in dealing with these problems. In particular, the model guides us to

1. identify what we know;
2. suggest alternative ways of responding based on sound conceptual thinking;
3. build in reflection as a key element in judging success;
4. retool the organization to manage the tasks; and
5. based on the success of the program, notify others of its application.

In this approach, we include a significant temporal component, showing that the actions that are taken have consequences that need to be considered in future tasks.

RISK ASSESSMENT

Assessing Uncertainties, Threats, and Hazards

Drawing from the assessment of risk, and emerging from the model of risk that we discussed earlier in this chapter, we focus on the elements of uncertainty, threat, and hazard. In looking at the role of policing in dealing with these types of issues, there is a great deal of ambiguity in the environment. It is not clear how effective arrests are in reducing crime; for example, while offenders are known to police in one context (drug dealing), it is not always predictable who will become violent, and so on. We can reduce uncertainty through a more detailed understanding of the individuals and communities that we are studying and the threats that they pose to social order. This uncertainty can be dealt with through better surveillance and intelligence, in addition to better data about past crimes (location, offender/victim relationship, etc.). The reliance on arrest data can cause some difficulties in assessing risk as this presumes that all offenders who pose threats are eventually arrested—clearly this is not the case. At a minimum, though, we might presume that arrested individuals represent a cross-section of those who might be offenders.

We then move from uncertainty, threat, and hazard to exposure, vulnerability, and incident, where an assessment needs to be done about how these elements led to criminal products. Without vulnerability and exposure, we are unlikely to experience crime. If offenders are not present, the risk of crime is obviously negligible. But we need, as well, to account for other unexpected factors, including the promotion of these crimes as a result of something like market demand for drugs or the resistance that comes from communities against allowing street crime to continue. An even more surprising outcome may be a decrease in violence that comes as drug gangs seek to reduce conflict as a way to remove the threat of police intervention that would disrupt drug transactions. We'll take these ideas and see how they would apply in our case study.

We begin at the assessment stage by constructing a risk model that combines the elements of micro and macro levels (activities of individuals and groups); locates them in a spatial area; and accounts for how they occur over time.

Uncertainty

1. What Can We Learn from Surveillance?

a. Formal Surveillance (by Police)

As is often the case, it is unclear who the main players are in the drug markets in this case-study community. Past arrests have identified the groups that are represented and have included some of the leadership. But the individuals on the street most directly involved in the day-to-day activities of the drug trade are the primary targets of surveillance. We know that certain areas are prime locations (based both on the arrest information and the targeted enforcement areas). The arrest data, when plotted on maps, present a picture of drug activity and violence throughout the town. Also, while it is clear that those who are arrested both belong to gangs and are spread throughout the town, it is not clear if gang members are the main players in the violence. Yet, with the increased clearance rates, this is becoming more evidently the case.

The risk assessment involves a plan to talk to local law enforcement and detectives about the crime activity. This type of information exchange would go a long way to reduce the uncertainty about who is involved. Drawing from the experiences of individuals who patrol an area and are in constant contact with individuals living there, we increase our understanding of what is going on. We are also able to make connections, identifying patterns in behavior that is difficult to do by individuals faced with the day-to-day demands of responding to problems.

b. Informal Surveillance (by the Public and Other Stakeholders—Agencies, and So Forth)

From the community members themselves, it is important, as well, to get a sense of the risks they see in their neighborhoods and the steps they take to protect themselves. This is a formidable requirement that may be beyond the resources of local officials, but some efforts (including community meetings) would go a long way to establish how the community is responding to the challenges it faces. In highly disorganized areas, communities may be hard to identify, and there may be great reluctance to get involved in discussions with authorities, but this information is critical to understanding stakeholders' views of the crime problem.

This search for and identification of risks extends to all participants, both directly and indirectly. We are interested, as well, in the hazards that participants in the drug trade themselves face and how they seek to reduce their risks. This can have the important effect of providing a better understanding of what the violence flash points are, but it also serves to make more sense out of how drug dealing and violent behavior relate to one another and the extent to which participants (both sellers and buyers) are willing to take chances to pursue these behaviors.

2. What Types of Environments Are We Working with, and What Can We Expect from These?

When we consider the hazards associated with these transactions, we need to consider not only who is involved but also the nature of the environments in which these activities take place. In our example, the area of greatest drug activity is a highly disorganized area surrounded by better organized towns. The population is poor and the local police are poorly managed. There is a great deal of housing vacancy and poor community services to provide alternatives to drug involvement. The street lighting is inadequate. In addition, there is a high concentration of illegal activity in certain locations, that is, hot spots, that are characterized as having both easy accessibility to highways (for the distribution of the goods) and the ability to fortify houses that serve as locations to hide drug stashes. Dealing with the vulnerability that comes from this type of neighborhood breakdown is difficult. It is hard, for example, to set up stakeouts to undertake surveillance. The physical design of these areas makes entry into and out of these locations by car difficult, making the activity of police easy to monitor. In addition, while it may seem obvious that, if we know where the drugs are we just go in and get them, this is actually more difficult than it sounds, particularly as the drugs may be distributed over a number of different addresses, requiring that separate search warrants be issued for each location. This makes the job of enforcement that much more difficult.

The physical decline in these areas, then, provides an ideal environment for these activities, making it difficult to provide surveillance and hard to patrol. Vacant houses with no clearly identified occupants can become havens for dealers and users with no official records available to track offenders. It is possible in these locations to work at excluding outsiders, if they can be identified, who might be coming to these locations to obtain the drugs. This is a hit or miss process, but this form of control may be the most effective in these types of circumstances.

Strategies

1. Narratives: Explaining What Is Known and What May Be Unknown Based on What Others Have Found
The first step in risk assessment is to identify the sources of uncertainty. What is known about the problem, and what is still unclear or unknowable? It is at this stage that investigators can develop a narrative that describes the sources of information and the general challenges faced in getting this information through surveillance and assistance from the community. The key players, as much as can be discerned from the information at hand, should be identified, and the challenges posed by the behavior and the locations need to be articulated. This provides an initial problem statement that sets the stage for the subsequent risk analysis.

2. Predictions about Likely Outcomes
The initial narrative should contain not only a description of the problem but also what the risk assessment judges to be the likely outcome of a failure to intervene. In these terms, the assessment lays out the difficulties that have been experienced in the past, for example. Importantly, at this stage, a general review of the effects of different types of police intervention (e.g., increased patrol and reduced access) that have been used in the past is necessary. Further, an analysis of the situation that includes a review of what would happen if the drug market were left alone should be undertaken. Is the drug market likely to expand, or will other factors, such as reduced demand, drive it out of business?

Hazards and Threats

1. Identifying Specific Hazards and Threats

Hazards and threats are, in practical terms, somewhat difficult to differentiate from one another. This stage moves specifically to addressing the actual incidents that occur and the interactions that take place between offenders, victims, and bystanders. The most important distinction is that hazards are what we currently face and threats are signs or symbols of negative events that could occur in the future. When we consider the hazards, we need to use information from a variety of sources, but the most immediate are the data provided from arrest reports. Now, we are not restricted to information on who is the offender. Arrest reports generally contain much more information. The offender's past criminal history is included as is information about the location of the crime and the nature of the offense. Information about the victim (if there is one) is included, in addition to the nature of the relationship between the parties, and where parties live (and, sometimes, other information such as gang affiliation and the presence of guns). All of this information provides important threat information, assuming that offenses will share certain characteristics, particularly if we are right in assuming that the locational characteristics attract certain crimes. So, this creates a picture of threat and creates a road map for how we would respond to future threats.

In addition, we have the intelligence that police officers collect from the community (beyond the narratives they might have from offenders and victims that go further than what is collected in police reports). The changing character of crime, the addition of new groups (buyers or sellers) to an area, and the playing out of intergroup conflict all become an important part of the threat assessment. But, these threats need to be considered in the context of the exposure and vulnerability evaluations. It is only on this basis that an understanding of the durability and seriousness of threats can be truly considered.

Also, we need to remember that crime problems themselves may interact with one another. For example, the rise in drug traffickers often leads to an increased risk of violence and a coexistence with prostitution. Now, while the drug markets might increase violence, robberies and prostitution may simply coexist with drug activity in highly disorganized communities but not, on the surface, appear to have anything to do with one another. In fact, however, the same people involved in one activity appear to often find their way into the other activities (people commit robberies to fuel their drug habits, prostitutes take clients to pay for drugs, and so on). So, the threats that come with one form of crime will increase threats associated with other activities. Interestingly, in the response to some crimes in certain areas, there may be complacency about low-level drug dealing or prostitution that disappears when these locations become violent. This type of interrelated threat picture is an important one both in understanding the extent and depth of the threat as well as understanding the degree to which law enforcement may be willing to act (and commit resources) to deal with these problems.

2. Conducting Behavioral Assessments

In extending this analysis, we can take advantage of the narrative information provided in police reports that explain what happened during crimes documented by police. The narrative includes commentary from offenders, victims, and witnesses (plus the police) and provides a review of the events that led up to and immediately followed the incident. Interestingly enough, these narratives are often ignored in research about crime as they are difficult for researchers to access, but, in addition, crime analysts rely more heavily on aggregated crime statistics than event information. With a well-designed event analysis, we should be able to supplement our understanding of the risk factors present in the area under consideration, in terms related to the hazards that these crimes pose.

3. Mining Data for Specific Threats

Beyond looking at the individual events that we can find in police reports, a good assessment requires that we identify patterns of behavior. An important aspect of threat and hazard identification connects to the concentration of crime in certain locations as identified by spatial analysis. Plotting the addresses of the crimes and comparing these provides us with an ability to chart hot spots, areas that attract both crime behavior and police attention. In using geographic information systems (GIS) technology, this hot spot analysis can point to density effects or identify patterns along transportation corridors. It can be mapped to identify changes over time (through the day or over the week). These changes can be compared to the patterns of police presence and can be connected to the sociodemographic characteristics of these areas. The risk potential that these maps can identify provides strategic guidance to police concerning where they should send their resources when working pro-actively to reduce crime. This hot spot analysis, of course, can be somewhat self-fulfilling, and the police can fall into the trap of creating dense locations of offenses based on their focus on certain areas over others. Over time, the patterns are useful in directing resources and also comparing time periods to establish successes in interventions.

The mapping of crime also provides some interesting insight into other risk factors: location of offenders and victims and the creation of cold spots. We are able, from arrest records, to plot the relative location of where offenders versus their victims live. This is important in establishing the degree to which offenders travel to crime and the extent to which living in proximity to offenders puts victims at risk. As for cold spots, as pointed out earlier, we discover that, even in areas of high crime, there exist locations in which there are few arrests or reports of criminal behavior. These low-risk areas may be characterized by residents with high home ownership where there is a strong commitment on the part of the inhabitants to discourage crime. It is important that we identify these areas as they provide a good deal of information about what it takes to keep a location crime free.

As we described earlier, "intelligence" is the acquisition of various forms of data to enable more accurate and focused assessments of where crime threats and hazards lie. The goal of intelligence gathering is to use this information to prevent the commission of criminal acts causing harm. Intelligence may therefore relate to either very specific sources or types of potential harm, or it may include information about more general types of threats. By implication, a challenge to intelligence gathering is to put abstract, or discrete, information together in unique ways in order to better identify where specific threats may lie. A recent example is that of Interpol (International Criminal Police Organization), which serves as a data repository for discrete types of information, and which recently facilitated putting together information used to identify a specific threat. According to one source, an offender had appeared in a large number of photographs abusing children, although the perpetrator's face had been digitally altered with a computer program that "swirled" the image. After unscrambling the images, the results were broadcast around the world, and after receiving many leads, the general threat was specifically identified, resulting in the offender's arrest.[1]

Strategies

1. Hot Spot Analysis

Central to the analysis of hazards is a spatial mapping of where crimes have occurred. As we pointed out, though, these hot spots can be deceptive, as they show congregations of events even though they may have occurred at very different times of the day or day of the week. With this caution, we can use these visual representations to offer a view of the distribution of hazards, providing the opportunity to match resource allocation to crime occurrence.

2. Crime Event Analysis

This step encourages us to reconstruct the crime incidents, using police reports, by adding context to them. This gives us a clear idea of what type of behavior it is we are trying to deter and the consequences that it is already having on the neighborhood.

MAKING CONNECTIONS

Exposure

1. Identify Networks and Relationships of Major Groups that Are Operating and Their General Practices

At this stage, we turn to the data that have been collected (from interviews and arrests) to provide us with information about who is likely to be involved in the drug trade and the subsequent (or attendant) violence. In our case study, we find that the major groups involved are part of street gangs mobilized to manage the drug trade. However, the information collected about victims of violence indicates that these individuals are not from these groups. This is an interesting finding, suggesting that the drug markets may be controlled by violent individuals, but the individuals who suffer from this violence are those who inhabit these neighborhoods but are not part of the market itself. They are victims of robberies, mostly, suggesting that the violence is instrumental in supporting the clients' needs for money to buy drugs rather than the sellers' needs to control the marketplace. This is not to say that the latter are not violent; their activity appears more likely to extend beyond the local boundaries of the study area.

The issue of exposure to violence is set in the context of the larger problem of drug crime and the extensive use of guns in locations where drugs are sold. The general patterns of drug movement and distribution are important. If there is a drop in demand, this will impact these local areas and the problems might change. In addition, if there are newly identified patterns in the movement of guns, this is important in our assessment of exposure to this type of violence. Where guns are not available, this may become less of a problem to deal with. In addition, we need to know what other types of factors might be playing a role in local problems, including the actions of major gangs and their plans for expanding their territories of influence.

Exposure may also be influenced by the characteristics of the individuals living in the affected area. If the area is predominantly poor, there will be problems with the individual resources that can be brought to bear against drug dealers and buyers. These residents will have more difficulty mobilizing the police against these criminals. Compounding this problem may be the difficulties faced by a highly transient group of young people who drift to these areas because they are cheap to live in. With scarce resources, these individuals are more susceptible to recruitment into drug activity, as either sellers or users.

2. Assess the Costs of the Crimes in Terms of Both Community and Police Resources

The costs of the crimes are hard to measure in real dollar terms, but there are other ways of measuring cost. These can include the change in neighborhood infrastructure (increased vacancy rates, declining average incomes, social disorder offenses, and so on). They may also be calculated in terms of the effects that insurance company policies have on the degree to which people can insure their homes or cars. Added costs to the township that come from repairs of infrastructure and the additional expense of providing secure schools for children need to be added to the calculation. These are not always easily translated from risk factors, but there is enough solid research (see Sampson and Raudenbush 1999) to show that areas that suffer from decline in these markers are also confounded by problems of crime and violence.

Added to this equation is the cost of providing an adequate police presence in these areas to respond to the crime problem. The paradox is that areas that have a high risk of offending are also likely to be the areas that have the least capacity to mount adequate law enforcement response to curtail these problems. So, if the problem becomes serious enough, as is true in our case study, the additional costs of adding state police to street enforcement must be added to the tally for law enforcement. Increased exposure, then, may be offset by more interventions, but these clearly come at a cost.

Strategies

At this stage in the assessment, we have to drill down to examine who the major groups are in the community that might be exposed to the problems of violence that come from living close to a drug market. The tasks that are prescribed at this stage include the following.

1. Careful Analyses of Active Groups and Their Actions and Interactions
The identification of gangs, past offenders, individuals who have been multiply victimized, and the types of crimes that occur (e.g., robberies and assaults) provide the information at this stage that is needed to make sense of who is at risk of victimization in these locations.

2. Descriptions of Past Events
A tally of past offenses will provide a chronicle of exposure across the neighborhood and suggest patterns of behavior that come as a consequence of the changing character of these locations. This can include an assessment of the degree to which there is a high level of quality of life offenses (tabulated through arrests or through police accounts of measures taken to deal with disorderly behavior).

3. Inventories of Policy Steps Taken to Manage Exposure to These Crimes
The strategies that have been used to address individuals' exposure to violence in these types of environments need to be addressed. For example, the use of programs such as Neighborhood Watch or Operation Ceasefire should be described along with their successes (and failures).

4. Accounting of Local Expenditures on Schools, Parks, Playgrounds, and Bus Stops, Particularly from a Regular Maintenance Perspective
Exposure may be influenced by the degree to which an area is neglected in terms of civic infrastructure. An area that receives less attention, running all the way from basic civic services to investments in recreational facilities and schools, provides a context in which social disorganization can prevail, increasing the likelihood that these areas become targets for drug dealers and their clients. With investment comes social capital, increasing the likelihood

that the community will take steps to make their neighborhoods more secure, and reducing the exposure to crime and violence.

5. Examination of the Resource Allocation for Local and State Police Personnel Assigned to These Communities (Compared to the Average Costs in Other Jurisdictions)

Tied to the commitment of infrastructure resources is the allocation of police resources. It may appear, on the surface, that communities will get the same level of service with increased expenditures on policing. This is simply not the case in poor, urban areas, and the problem is compounded by the difficulties that are encountered due to poor organization and limited training of officers. Supplementing these resources through the use of outside forces is one way to address this problem and to reduce the exposure that these communities face. However, this type of intervention is difficult and costly. This needs to be considered as part of the risk assessment.

Vulnerability

1. Target Identification

Vulnerability moves us from exposure to prospective analysis of the specific presence of key players who might participate in the crimes that we see developing in these areas. It also includes an assessment of the likelihood that victims will appear in this location. Most importantly, addressing vulnerability means focusing on the extent to which we can do something about reducing the likelihood that crime will occur based on the exposure factors laid out above. This leads to a series of questions we need to address:

1. If there are targets of crime, can they be protected or removed?
2. Can offenders be apprehended?
3. If there are locations that are riper for certain types of criminal activity, can they be altered to make them safer?
4. Can we restrict movement into and out of these areas to interrupt the flow of offenders (in the drug trade, both buyers and sellers) and victims (people who may be innocent bystanders who get attacked for money or for reasons of territorial control)?

In preparing for interventions, an important part of risk assessment relates to the identification of key players and their likely involvement in crime. For example, the drug trade contains certain individuals who take over its control and lead others to violence in maintaining territory. Understanding who these individuals are and, as importantly, who their rivals are can go a long way to control the trade and reduce violence. As an example of this, there was a recent story of two gang members (who were brothers) who were thought to be influential in the drug trade in a local neighborhood of a major city. These two had been arrested for violent crimes, in addition to having warrants out for their arrest related to selling drugs. At the same time, a major rival was about to be released from prison, and the worry on the part of the police was that, once free, the rival would seek to take out his opponents and reclaim the drug market. The police moved quickly to reduce this risk by rounding up the brothers, ensuring that, in the short run at least, violence would be avoided.

Identifying others involved in these activities, including customers for drugs or prostitution, is more difficult as they are often free of arrest records and may only be sporadic visitors to a neighborhood (unlike the suppliers who are more likely to reside there). Identifying individuals who are in the wrong place at the wrong time puts the police in an awkward position relative to privacy and freedom of movement, but discouraging individuals from coming to an area to purchase drugs would help to both reduce the likelihood that this trade would continue and provide fewer targets for violent victimization in these locations.

In doing this type of vulnerability assessment, we pay close attention to how context affects behavior that occurs in these areas. This includes a clear understanding that vulnerability is not constant across time or place but can vary by time of day or day of the week. Also, it can move, in response to law enforcement pressure or market demand, from one location to another. The situational prevention ideas that evolve from this assessment, then, address how we might alter this vulnerability quotient: removing opportunity, addressing the key factors that might lower the risk of victimization, and raising the costs of offending.

2. Assessment of Likelihood of Success

When we address the plans for prevention and reduction of risk, we need to consider the ways in which we can judge the success of our interventions. Moving barricades across streets or locking up drug houses are perfectly sensible responses to restricting drug trade. But, do they in fact reduce this activity or do they simply it someplace else? In considering these responses and their impact on vulnerability reduction, we need to consider how to evaluate these activities. This is more difficult than it seems, a point we will make again when we discuss risk management strategies. If we look at passive responses, such as blocking street access, we don't have real measures of change (short of sitting and watching over time how the drug traffic changes, for example).

So, we are forced to rely on crude measures of change, such as, do we notice a decline over time in the number of drug arrests in an area while not observing a similar increase elsewhere? Similarly, it is difficult to track law enforcement interventions closely as police are rarely programmed to the point where their hourly movement is predetermined and tracked. They go to an area and then operate through a general pattern of patrol, a pattern that may be difficult to track.

3. Level of Damage

Vulnerability must also be considered in the context of how far along the damage is that has been done to the social and physical infrastructure of a community when the interventions begin. If there is no operating community, if the streets are poorly lit, if the schools are in disarray, and if the parks are unsafe, this means that the risks of crime are higher and the likelihood of success in introducing situational prevention strategies is greatly reduced. This problem has made certain communities long-standing locations of problems, even when there is a steady flow of different people into and out of a community (a problem identified by Clifford Shaw and Henry McKay in specific problem neighborhoods in Chicago seventy years ago). Understanding this long-standing problem with disorder is important in dealing with those locations that seem most vulnerable. There is a form of self-fulfilling prophecy that develops around these communities that keeps them from engaging in self-help and makes policy makers and police more reluctant to invest greater resources into areas that already seem to be unsalvageable. This is the greatest challenge faced in offsetting this problem.

Strategies

1. Tactical Assessment of Target Protection Methods

At this stage in the assessment, the specific value of certain types of intervention (e.g., patrol, arrest, and access control) needs to be considered in terms of their practicality but also their likely success in reducing the vulnerability in the affected neighborhood.

2. Resources Needed to Mitigate Damage

These tactics need to reflect the reality in the areas being targeted and be reasonable in light of the resources available for deployment. If the local police are unable to deal with this vulnerability, other agencies will need to be deployed. However, the decisions that are made about when and how this will take place sometimes occur after serious problems have already set into a location. This uncovers one of the real problems that the assessments intend to head off, that is, arriving too late with too little. However, it is inevitable that problems will need to be at a level that attracts special attention if we continue to follow reactive policing strategies. By requiring a proactive approach through risk assessment, some of the difficulties that derive from arriving too late, when the vulnerability levels are already high, can be addressed.

3. Inventory of Vulnerable Areas and History of Crime Problems
This leads to the suggestion that this form of risk assessment be transportable, that is, that a standardized process be implemented that would allow and encourage agencies to more strategically compare vulnerabilities according to an established set of guidelines. This sharing of resources and a more concerted effort work to reduce vulnerabilities.

Causation

Using the assessment strategies, we search for underlying theoretical causal explanations related to crime emergence. It is here that we search for the cause/effect components of the risk problem and different forms of preparedness and prevention. At this stage we decide whether or not we will approach the risk problem as one of opportunity reduction or a focus on clearing out offenders from an area. We might consider a more broad-scale approach such as concentrating on dealing with the problems of social disorder, which might involve community programs (community crime-prevention plans) or neighborhood cleanup drives. Regardless of what is decided, the intervention needs to articulate the underlying assumptions and must be guided by the information that is collected from the initial risk assessments. It is important that whatever explanation for the problem's occurrence and for the solution offered is supported by a clear set of analytical principles and testable assumptions. When an explanation is used, risk evaluation needs to connect this back to an underlying theory (just as we did through our discussions in the preceding chapters). This provides rigor in outlining the risk-reduction strategies and managing resources in an expeditious manner. This is not to say, as we pointed out in our discussion of the three stages of risk in chapter 1, that we cannot use more than one theory. We can, but we need to ensure that the theories used are not contradictory and are fully explicated. A proper implementation and evaluation requires this level of specificity.

As explained in chapter 2, the broken windows perspective is an attempt to use surveillance as a means of addressing issues of uncertainty. This approach deals primarily with abstract threats given that the idea behind broken windows is to respond to a variety of disorderly behaviors with a view to halting or preventing more serious criminal behaviors—criminal behaviors as yet undefined. The broken windows perspective makes the assumption that, by addressing a range of disorder-type issues, whatever those might be, these efforts will inhibit the commission of other crimes.

It is important to provide some further clarification with respect to how we view the broken windows perspective and its relationship to precursor, transaction, and aftermath. The broken windows perspective is clearly an anticipatory perspective—uncertainty in the precursor stage drives various activities geared toward preventing exposure to serious criminal behavior. The anticipation of being exposed to serious harm propels this perspective. What is difficult to measure, as we noted earlier, is whether any of the anticipatory actions taken to address a range of disorderly behaviors actually serve to reduce the exposure to more serious activity. A health-related analogy is helpful here. "Exposure" may refer to a range of activities that are likened to a syndrome—a conglomeration of disorderly offenses that signify an underlying issue: propensity to serious crime. Initiating preventative action to address these various symptoms will ensure that a syndrome (serious crime) will not develop.

The idea behind situational crime prevention is that there are specific, identifiable hazards in the environment that must be taken into account in order to reduce the likelihood of criminal victimization. The identification of hazards and threats is based upon past experience and research. For example, victimization and policing data indicate that bars pose specific hazards. Aside from eliminating the bar, various measures can be taken to address the hazards associated with these establishments: regulated and enforced closing times, limits on drink orders, private security, food service, and so forth. This approach includes elements of situational prevention and represents the arguments put forward by Clarke and Newman (2006).

Then, there are more general connections that move us from surveillance and opportunity reduction to an emphasis on social problems that create increased crime probability in particular areas. As we have discussed, these tend to emphasize vulnerability and exposure in certain groups that comes from heightened victimization.

The ways in which these issues are addressed depends entirely on the goals and objectives of the agencies as well as on the resources that agencies have available to them. Policing agencies that profess a law and order approach may be less concerned with crime prevention (the precursor stage) and more concerned with the specific hazard itself and their responses to it. While it may be overgeneralizing to suggest that first responders are concerned exclusively with responding to specific types of hazards, responders prioritize as their name suggests—*responding* to crises. There are clearly also a number of policing agencies that work toward prevention. Agencies that align with a community policing perspective have prevention squarely in mind in many of their undertakings. Those that focus on punishment will have, as a primary focus, the arrest and incarceration of offenders.

Strategies

1. Analyzing data for trends and patterns
2. Making connections between vulnerabilities and consequences
3. Creating explanations for crime outcomes
4. Applying and developing theories about crime occurrence, including, for example,
   - opportunity theory,
   - social disorganization, and
   - social control
5. Intelligence reports on crime problems
6. Audits of success of intervention programs

SETTING TASKS TO RESPOND AND PREVENT

Prevention, Preparedness, and Response

1. Identify Ways of Mitigating Risk through Prevention

When a strategy has been decided on to provide intervention and reduce risk, there is a need to assign tasks to be completed to get the job done. In our example, the local police may have limited ability to go after the offenders, but they can take part in surveillance that is important for gathering information about crime hot spots. The police can be deployed in crime areas in a way that ensures they are there when the crime occurs, not at a time that is convenient to their patrol schedules. Other agencies may be useful in discouraging drug activity with reporting from schools, bus drivers, and others as a way of targeting certain areas. This process needs to be coordinated. It is increasingly the case that closed-circuit television (CCTV) is being deployed in problem areas. Active rather than passive use of this technology in managing public areas may afford an important new resource in the reduction of risk.

2. Develop General and Specific Intervention Programs that Confront Underlying Problems, as Well as Prescribe Specific Responses

The job of the police is not just to make arrests after the fact but also to encourage order. Working with other agencies in troubled locations (including probation and parole, school officials, and community groups) allows a better coordination of response. There have been a number of efforts at this type of reaction (we have talked about these programs that range from Neighborhood Watch to more specific violence intervention programs, such as Operation Ceasefire). These programs are based on certain assumptions about how crime occurs and can be stopped, but as importantly, they provide a clear set of guidelines concerning who should do what in prevention and response. This task assignment is a key element in any risk management program that is implemented.

Strategies

1. Prevention Programs Specifically Tied to Vulnerabilities and Threats
Whatever plan is adopted, the key elements need to relate to the vulnerabilities and threats that are experienced in the community being addressed. Introducing programs that are not clearly tied to these issues is an exercise that is likely to fail.

2. Ongoing Target Hardening
Community involvement plans and strategies to improve neighborhoods must include mechanisms that will provide greater local security. A conscientious plan that emphasizes target hardening, making victims less vulnerable and providing them with more protection, needs to be a priority in any risk management plan.

3. Recovery Plans
To achieve success in reducing vulnerabilities, there needs to be an accompanying plan to assist in dealing with the negative consequences of previous victimization. If there is no longer-term recovery plan, one that sustains the successes of the attack on crime, the likelihood of a return to the problems is greatly enhanced.

COLLECTING INFORMATION ABOUT THE EVENT

Evaluation

Key to the successful completion of a risk management plan is a well-organized information system that provides data about exposure and vulnerability but also permits ongoing evaluation of the success of various interventions. As already mentioned, it is sometimes difficult to collect detailed information about police movements beyond arrest data. However, with a clearly articulated set of goals defined in the plan, the required data can be identified and efforts made to collect it. In particular, the task of a good evaluation involves establishing whether or not the intervention that took place actually worked. We are not only looking at the state of the crime problem but are interested, as well, in the changes that ment in these communities. In our case study, we want to know that crime is decreasing, but also we want to know how effective agencies other than the police are in returning the community to order and security. Sustaining this and monitoring whether or not other areas in the community are turned into drug markets requires an ongoing evaluation of the success of the interventions.

Measuring and attributing causal effects can be difficult, although in a well-established "process review," the stated objectives (e.g., a decline in crime by a set amount) can be assessed. More sophisticated evaluation can include quasi-experimental designs where areas are selected for treatment and compared to areas that are not. If the areas are well matched, any change in the crime problem should then be attributed to the intervention. This type of evaluation design is desirable from an analysis point of view but is difficult to introduce in areas where the crime problem is serious, requiring that all areas are treated the same in terms of police response. However, as has been done in some well-known police evaluations, it is possible, if not to remove intervention, then to alter the strategies that are used in pursuing the crime. Evaluations can provide important information on the variations in causal effects (e.g., enhanced street patrols versus targeted arrests) of these different approaches.

Connected to this evaluation process is the need for an increasingly sophisticated information gathering and analysis planning. Police agencies, for years, have suffered from both poor and stale information as well as the inability to connect information sources together to identify trends and provide leads. With the coming of data fusion centers, the possibility of tying together these records is greatly enhanced. This provides a major step forward in identifying and pursuing crime risks.

Strategies

1. Evaluation of Risk Management Strategies
Objectives, goals, and measurable outcomes are necessary to ensure that intervention and crime-reduction strategies have worked.

2. Intelligence Feedback in Event Analysis
Sharing information reduces the probability of difficult circumstances repeating themselves, with a feedback cycle recognizing that the aftermath of one event becomes the precursor stage to another event.

REFINING THE ORGANIZATION

Risk governance requires that an organization shift its focus away from a truly reactive stance to one that is more proactive. In this way, it becomes a knowledge-based enterprise that relies on information about its current functioning and its environment to set goals, to evaluate actions, and to plan its resources. In a risk model, the primary intention in using a proactive approach is to mitigate and reduce risk. This pertains both to the organization and to those whom the organization serves. As we have noted, when talking to police, they will say that they work with risk models, but they just don't call these by this name. Instead, they rarely conduct systematic risk assessments, and they tend to make haphazard use of information to judge the success of their plans. When the assessment is done, it is most often performed using crude measures (such as crime rates) that represent only one form of risk (albeit an important one) and that may be dated by the time the information is collated and evaluated. Turning police departments into risk management organizations may not be too hard to do given the recent receptivity to intelligence-led policing, which, combined with ideas about risk balance, will encourage accountability of actions and resources. To make this work, police leadership must begin to think in terms of risk factors and priorities and send a clear signal to the rest of the organization of the value of evidence-based decision making in planning risk abatement strategies.

Strategies

1. Developing a monitoring capacity within the organization
2. Setting out guidelines for reporting relations
3. Developing accountability schemes
4. Lines of authority
5. Strategic and tactical decision making
6. Education and training in risk management

NOTIFYING OTHERS

Creating Awareness and Risk Communication

An important aspect of risk governance is the role that risk communication plays in defining goals and imparting to others the strategic plans of the organization. As important, the organization (in this case law enforcement) has an obligation to explain to the community that it identifies and deals with hazards and threats faced within its jurisdiction, as well as communicating the steps that are being taken to mitigate these risks. Obviously, as we have stated, the conversation around risk will be influenced by fear and may lead to demands that are hard to meet or not realistic given the threats and hazards that are faced. But, with the help of a clearly stated risk plan, these fears may be directly addressed and managed. As has happened in our case study, successes have to be communicated. The hiring of a new police chief has been identified as a way of increasing the organizational efficiency of the local police. His first task, he said, was to address the ways in which the police function and then to examine how they could be more successful in addressing the crime problem.

So, as important as fear is, the organization needs to communicate the steps that it is taking to address the source of these fears (perceptions of threat and hazard). These may include the development of risk manuals for specific events or narratives that explain the steps that are being taken to deal with crime problems. Obviously, a key part of the communication process involves dealings with the media. This interaction is often difficult as the media see their job as reporting on crime not on policing. The complexities of risk assessment and risk management strategies may not fit into the day-to-day accounts of crime statistics. But the advantage of having clearly informed decisions that back up responses to the risks that have been documented would go a long way to provide context in which the media can judge the likelihood of success of intervention and the long-term prospects for the problems faced in problem neighborhoods.

Strategies

1. Risk manuals
2. Community awareness programs
3. Current organizational status

A CAVEAT: ETHICAL CONCERNS IN USING RISK MEASURES

The call for risk assessments obviously derives from a concern that we more clearly understand the total picture when we take action against crime. Yet, we also need to be aware that risk assessments can become tools that can be used unfairly against certain groups seen as being highly dangerous. The assessments should not be offered as an excuse to put pressure on communities in a way that assumes they will be troublesome, without providing alternatives and continued monitoring (or accountability) within the assessments. As an example, efforts at detaining minority drivers on the state turnpikes in anticipation that they would be more likely to be carrying drugs created a type of profiling that led to serious violations of the rights and liberties of individuals classified into these groups but innocent of this behavior (see Steven Bernstein's [1990] discussion of Operation Pipeline that was promoted as a way of targeting drug couriers but ended up being severely criticized for encouraging racial profiling). In addition, care must be taken to reinforce the idea that risk assessments should be reviewed by someone with expertise in an area, holding the framers of the document accountable to certain standards of evidence. Without this, mistakes can be made that will be a problem for future initiatives.

There is, as well, an unanticipated problem with risk assessments that showed up in a recently adjudicated case surrounding the first bombing of the World Trade Center in New York City in 1993. Prior to the bombing taking place, the police had initiated an exhaustive review of the buildings' vulnerabilities to further attack. They issued a risk assessment, in 1985, which indicated that, if certain steps were not taken, the building would come under attack, in particular the parking garage under the building that posed a particularly high risk for attack. When the bomb went off, the steps that had been outlined in the report had not been taken, and a number of victims and the family of victims brought suit against the owner of the buildings (the Port Authority of New York and New Jersey) for negligence in not following the recommendations, increasing the likelihood that the attack would be successful.

After many years of litigation, a judge pronounced that the complainants were justified in their suit and found against the owners, suggesting they were 68 percent responsible for the attacks through failure to prevent them (while the bombers were 32 percent responsible), meaning that the Port Authority would be responsible for 100 percent of the damages sought by litigants. In other words, the owners were held responsible for not following through on the suggestions made in the risk assessment. This illustrates the challenges in undertaking these types of initiatives (Hartocollis 2008).

At the same time, it is as likely that one would be held responsible if a risk assessment had not been done. As we see with the increased pressure on schools and universities to develop emergency response plans that account for a number of different contingencies, including fire, attacks on students, and so on, there is little choice now but to put these plans in place. But, the job does not end there. The plans need to be feasible and actionable. The risks that are identified need to be addressed and, where possible, mitigated. But, of course, it is not always possible to fully accomplish this. This is where we move into the realm of risk balance.

ANOTHER CAVEAT: RISK BALANCE AND "ACCEPTABLE RISK"

In our book *Risk Balance and Security* (2008), we suggest that the concerns about risk in areas that include crime but also terrorism, environmental disaster, and health problems need to be considered in light of what we think we can actually do about responding to them. Importantly, in that approach, we considered what risk meant for security. As we point out in our application of risk balance, the determination of the nature of the response will be based on the resources we have available. This may limit what we can do, exposing us to the possibility that we cannot do enough. But, it also encourages us to set priorities and determine "acceptable" levels of risk, where not all chances of incidents go away but we move to a level that we find matches the resources we are willing to assign to the problem. In the crime context, we realize that crime will never completely go away (as is the case with disease or environmental threats), but the damage that it can do can be reduced, as we suggested in our initial discussion in chapter 1 about the likelihood of us ever completely eradicating murder.

If we cannot be completely secure, can we find a way of "getting back to normal" and returning to routines in the aftermath of crime? Before harm strikes, we build routines and manage our lives to ensure security. "Returning" to normal may well involve establishing a new normal. Factors come together to create conditions for an incident to occur; the incident is a reflection of an act that occurs in a specific time and place; and this act has consequences that govern how victims, law enforcement, criminal justice agencies, and communities react and attempt to change conditions so that the act cannot be repeated.

Risk balance defines how different elements are related and how these concepts help to create various security (or insecurity) outcomes. Security may then be achieved when hazards are balanced with resources, yet the balance changes depending on the temporal phase of (exposure to) the hazard. It is the challenge of risk assessment to find this balance and set guidelines for the future management of crime. Borrowing from our discussion in *Risk Balance and Security*, we propose a set of principles that guide how risk balance is negotiated.

1. Choice

We do not have access to infinite resources to address all of the threats that we face in modern life. Priorities are then selected for action. Choices, however, are not made in a social vacuum. The ability to direct resources to respective hazards does not always mean that resources will in fact be applied. Social and political factors play a role in decision making and the willingness to prioritize preparedness, response, and prevention measures to identified hazards. Importantly, for many of the hazards faced, choices can be made in advance to minimize harm.

2. Decision Making

A central theme running throughout our discussion is the need to make decisions about risk balance based on information. Information is central to risk balance: resources are typically allocated on the basis of what is known. Information is one distinct type of resource. While the unknown (either due to a lack of imagination or lack of resources) also figures into decision making, information is typically a required element influencing how seriously threats are perceived. It must also be noted, however, that having correct information does not necessarily imply particular action. Information alone will not ensure that smart decisions are made. It may simply increase the probability of harm reduction.

Good decision making relies on us having trust in sources of information. If the information source is not trusted, it is unlikely that this information will figure into assessments of risk—information is really only as good as its source. Not only are decisions based on information and trust, but decisions are also influenced by the availability of resources. If individuals recognize that they live in an area with high levels of burglaries—they have the information and trust the source of that information—the decisions that are made with respect to that threat must be weighed against (other) resources available. Those who have less economic resources, for example, may determine that, while they recognize the threat, they haven't the financial means to remove themselves from harm's way.

3. Cooperation

Effective decision making requires cooperation across groups that have not dealt with one another in an easy fashion or that suspect one another in the ongoing battle over jurisdictional turf. Developing a common language with respect to security may be difficult, but the contributions of risk balance suggest that problem solving, which manages tough decisions and forces resource choices, should become a central part of the security lexicon. Further, it is critical that security is not seen as a zero-sum game: the bolstering of security in one realm or by one actor does not necessarily diminish security in another realm for others. Similarly, bolstering security in one realm does not automatically enhance security in other realms.

4. Planning

Planning for crime prevention needs to extend beyond treating one type of hazard as completely different from another, while accepting that different hazards require focused responses. For agencies involved in emergency planning, for example, practice prepares for a quick and decisive response. But, this is not the end of the story. Success extends to preparation for the next incident based on lessons quickly learned from the recent incident. It also depends on the level of preparation that was put in place prior to the incident that may have mitigated the damage or quickened the response. CCTV did not deter the first set of bombs in London, but it quickly helped unravel the cause of the bombs leading to the suspects. As importantly, it became a vital tool in the dragnet that was set out in pursuit of the second set of unsuccessful bombers who were tracked down quickly after their failed attack. While planning is important and comes from practice, in order to be effective, plans must be well formed, pertinent, and involve all stakeholders affected by potential hazards. Planning is central to all stages of hazards, from the preparatory stage to the response and recovery stages.

5. Institutional Learning

The institutional learning of government agencies can facilitate a more competent response, contain the damage, and assist in quicker responses. Threats to our security are tied to one another, and our responses are based on innovating around routines that we have learned in managing risk in our everyday lives. Some of the daily prevention activities that we engage in provide model behavior for reducing potential harm. Much can be borrowed in our discussion of risk and security from the models drawn from, for example, how we view insurance as a device that encourages prevention and mitigates the costs of hazards.

6. Communication

The mobilization of resources to prepare for, respond to, and recover from hazards is dependent upon communication both within and between jurisdictions. By communication, we mean the process of both informing stakeholders of the hazards that affect them and, in turn, listening to stakeholders regarding their perceptions of and experiences with hazards. The Environmental Protection Agency (EPA) provides advice for risk communication, starting with rather basic first steps: determine what the message is that needs to be communicated and then deliver the message in a way that goals will be met. The EPA then suggests answering the following questions as a means of maximizing the effectiveness of hazards communication. As can be seen, these questions can apply to a range of hazardous situations: "Why are we communicating? Who are our target audiences? What do our audiences want to know? What do we want to get across? How will we communicate? How will we listen? How will we respond? Who will carry out the plans? When? What problems or barriers have we planned for? Have we succeeded?" (Environmental Protection Agency 2002). These questions assume that communication about hazards is at least a two-way street: stakeholders are encouraged to ask questions and provide feedback, while those providing information are encouraged to listen.

SUMMING UP

Over time and through space, the constitution of hazards changes: hazards that are viewed as only abstract possibilities at time 1 are viewed much differently at time 2 when abstractions become inevitabilities. Similarly, resources that were scarce at time 1 may be reallocated at time 2 with a far greater sense of urgency. Further, we have moved from focusing on crime hazards and threats as individual concerns to a consideration of crime hazards from a risk balance point of view, where risk assessment is contextualized in the lives of individuals and the actions of institutions and states that come to terms in different ways with particular hazards.

We considered how temporal and spatial positions relative to the identified crime hazard come into play to influence the probability of crime occurrence. The passage of time may bring us either closer to or further away from identified hazards and threats, influencing how we perceive the probability of future events. Our approach has suggested that to impact the probability of crime requires taking into account and balancing a number of factors. But, like anything else that is balanced, crime probabilities may be easily destabilized (if only by degree and by perspective) when or if certain factors weigh more than previously, or factors not taken into account previously suddenly figure into the crime equation differently than before.

NOTE

1. Interpol, "Thai Court Jails Pedophile Arrested after Interpol Global Appeal," at www.interpol.int/Public/THB/vico/Default.asp (accessed July 2008).

References

Abbott, A. 1997. Of time and space: The contemporary relevance of the Chicago school. *Social Forces* 75 (4): 1149–82.

Agnew, R. 2006. Storylines as a neglected cause of crime. *Journal of Research in Crime and Delinquency* 43 (2): 119–47.

Akins, S., C. Mosher, T. Rotolo, and R. Griffin. 2003. Patterns and correlates of substance use among American Indians in Washington State. *Journal of Drug Issues* 33 (1): 45–71.

Anderson, K. L. 2007. Who gets out? Gender as structure and the dissolution of violent heterosexual relationships. *Gender and Society* 21 (2): 173–201.

Andreas, P. 2003. *The rebordering of North America: Integration and exclusion in a new security context.* New York: Routledge.

Armstrong, D., J. Hine, S. Hacking, R. Armaos, R. Jones, N. Klessinger, and A. France. 2005. *Children, risk and crime: The On Track Youth Lifestyles Surveys.* Home Office Research Study 278. London: Home Office Research, Development and Statistics Directorate.

Baer, J., and W. J. Chambliss. 1997. Generating fear: The politics of crime reporting. *Crime, Law, and Social Change* 27 (2): 87–108.

Balkin, S. 1979. Victimization rates, safety, and fear of crime. *Social Problems* 26:343–58.

Baron, S. W., D. R. Forde, and L. W. Kennedy. 2007. Disputatiousness, aggressiveness, and victimization among street youths. *Youth Violence and Juvenile Justice* 5 (4): 411–25.

Bayley, D. H. 2008. Police reform: Who done it? *Policing and Society: An International Journal of Research and Policy* 18 (1): 7–17.

Beck, U. 1992. *Risk Society.* London: Sage.

Bedarf, A. R. 1995. Examining sex offender community notification laws. *California Law Review* 83 (3): 885–940.

Beirne, P., and J. Messerschmidt. 2000. *Criminology*. 3rd ed. Boulder, Colo.: Westview Press.

Bennett, T., K. Holloway, and D. P. Farrington. 2006. Does neighborhood watch reduce crime? A systematic review and meta-analysis. *Journal of Experimental Criminology* 2 (4): 437–58.

Bernstein, S. K. 1990. Fourth amendment: Using the drug courier profile to fight the war on drugs. *Journal of Criminal Law and Criminology* 80 (4): 996–1017.

Best, J. 1990. *Threatened children: Rhetoric and concern about child-victims*. Chicago: University of Chicago Press.

Blank, D. 2007. Reducing the risk of crime in your store. Expert Business Source, February 25, at www.expertbusinesssource.com/article/CA6419428.html (accessed April 2008).

Blee, K. M. 2007. The microdynamics of hate violence: Interpretive analysis and implications for responses. *American Behavioral Scientist* 51 (2): 258–70.

Block, R. L., and C. R. Block. 1995. Space, place, and crime: Hot spot areas and hot places of liquor-related crime. In *Crime and place: Crime prevention studies*, ed. J. E. Eck and D. Weisburd, 145–84. Crime Prevention Studies 4. Monsey, N.Y.: Criminal Justice Press.

Blumstein, A., and J. Cohen. 1987. Characterizing criminal careers. *Science* 237 (4818): 985–91.

Booth, C. 1879. *Life and labour of the people of London: First series: Poverty*. London.

Bouffard, J. A., and L. R. Muftic. 2007. An examination of the outcomes of various components of a coordinated community response to domestic violence by male offenders. *Journal of Family Violence* 22 (6): 353–66.

Braga, A., J. McDevitt, and G. Pierce. 2006. Understanding and preventing gang violence: Problem analysis and response development in Lowell. *Massachusetts Police Quarterly* 9 (1): 20–46.

Brantingham, P., and P. Brantingham. 1981. *Environmental criminology*. Beverly Hills, Calif.: Sage.

——. 1995. Criminality of place: Crime generators and crime attractors. *European Journal on Criminal Policy and Research* 3 (3): 1–26.

Bratton, W., and G. Kelling. 2006. There are no cracks in the broken windows: Ideological academics are trying to undermine a perfectly good idea. *National Review Online*, February 28, at www.nationalreview.com/comment/bratton_kelling 200602281015.asp (accessed May 6, 2009).

Bratton, W., and P. Knobler. 1998. *Turnaround: How America's top cop reversed the crime epidemic*. New York: Random House.

British Security Industry Association. 2001. Free helpline cures security headaches. News centre. May 8, at www.bsia.co.uk/ (accessed July 2008).

Bureau of Justice Statistics. 2006. Four measures of serious violent crime. U.S. Department of Justice, Office of Justice Programs, at www.ojp.usdoj.gov/bjs/glance/tables/4meastab.htm (accessed June 2009).

Byrne, C. A., D. G. Kilpatrick, and S. S. Howley. 1999. Female victims of partner versus nonpartner violence: Experiences with the criminal justice system. *Criminal Justice and Behavior* 26 (3): 275–92.

Campbell Collaborative. The Campbell Collaboration: What helps? What harms? Based on what evidence, at www.campbellcollaboration.org/ (accessed July 2008).

Carolan, M. S. 2007. The precautionary principle and traditional risk assessment: Rethinking how we assess and mitigate environmental threats. *Organization and Environment* 20 (1): 5–24.

Clarke, R. V. 1997. Introduction. In *Situational crime prevention: Successful case studies*, ed. R. V. Clarke, 1–42. 2nd ed. Guilderland, N.Y.: Harrow and Heston.

Clarke, R. V., and G. Newman. 2006. Can the police outsmart the terrorists? Paper presented at the annual meeting of the American Society of Criminology, Los Angeles, Calif., November.

———. 2006. *Outsmarting the terrorists*. London: Praeger Security International.

Corteen, K. 2002. Lesbian safety talk: Problematizing definitions and experiences of violence, sexuality and space. *Sexualities* 5 (3): 259–80.

Craig, L. A., A. Beech, and K. D. Browne. 2006. Cross-validation of the risk matrix 2000 sexual and violent scales. *Journal of Interpersonal Violence* 21 (5): 612–33.

Davenport, J. 2007. *Global extremism and terrorism*. New York: Chelsea House.

Davis, R. C., and B. Smith. 1994. Teaching victims crime prevention skills: Can individuals lower their risk of crime? *Criminal Justice Review* 19 (1): 56–68.

DeLisi, M. 2005. *Career criminals in society*. Thousand Oaks, Calif.: Sage.

DiUlio, J. 1995. The coming of the super-predators. *Weekly Standard*, November 27, 1995.

Douglas, M. 1966. *Purity and danger: An analysis of concepts of pollution and taboo*. London: Routledge and Kegan Paul.

Duff, A., and D. Garland. 1994. *A reader on punishment*. Oxford: Oxford University Press.

Eck, J. E. 1993. The threat of crime displacement. *Problem Solving Quarterly* 6 (3): 1–2.

———. 1995. A general model of the geography of illicit retail marketplaces. In *Crime and place: Crime prevention studies*, ed. J. E. Eck and D. Weisburd, 67–95. Crime Prevention Studies 4. Monsey N.Y.: Criminal Justice Press.

———. 1997. Preventing crime at places. In *Preventing crime: What works, what doesn't, what's promising. A report to the United States Congress*, ed. L. W. Sherman, 7-1–7-77. Washington, D.C.: U.S. Department of Justice.

———. 2001. Policing and crime event concentration. In *The process and structure of crime: Criminal events and crime analysis*, ed. R. Meier, L. Kennedy, and V. Sacco, 249–327. New Brunswick, N.J.: Theoretical Advances.

Eck, J. E., S. Chainey, J. Cameron, M. Leitner, and R. Wilson. 2005. *Mapping crime: Understanding hot spots*. Washington D.C.: U.S. Department of Justice, National Institute of Justice.

Eck, J. E., and D. Weisburd. 1995. *Crime and place: Crime prevention studies*. Mosney, N.Y.: Criminal Justice Press.

Edwards, A., and G. Hughes. 2005. Comparing the governance of safety in Europe: A geo-historical approach. *Theoretical Criminology* 9 (3): 345–63.

Ekici, N., M. Ozkan, A. Celik, and M. Maxfield. 2008. Outsmarting terrorists in Turkey. *Crime Prevention and Community Safety* 10 (2): 126–39.

Environmental Protection Agency (EPA). 2002. Risk communication. September, at www.epa.gov/superfund/community/pdfs/37riskcom.pdf (accessed May 6, 2009).

Ericson, R. 2005. Governing through risk and uncertainty. *Economy and Society* 34 (4): 659–72.

Ericson, R., and K. Haggerty. 1997. *Policing the risk society.* Toronto: University of Toronto Press.

European Institute for Crime Prevention and Control. Developing mechanisms for assessing the risk of crime due to legislation and products in order to proof them against crime at an EU level (MARC), at www.heuni.fi/36851.htm (accessed July 2008).

Ewald, U. 2000. Criminal victimization and social adaptation in modernity: Fear of crime and risk perception in the New Germany. In *Crime, risk, and insecurity: Law and order in everyday life and political discourse*, ed. T. Hope and R. Sparks, 166–99. London: Routledge.

Farrell, G., and K. Pease. 1993. Once bitten, twice bitten: Repeat victimization and its implications for crime prevention. Police Research Group Crime Prevention Unit Series Paper No. 46. London: Home Office Police Department.

Farrell, G., C. Phillips, and K. Pease. 1995. Like taking candy: Why does repeat victimization occur? *British Journal of Criminology* 35 (3): 384–99.

Farrell, G., and W. Souza. 2001. Repeat victimization and hot spots: The overlap and its implications for crime control and problem-oriented policing. *Crime Prevention Studies* 12:221–40.

Felson, R. B., and P. P. Pare. 2007. Gender and the victim's experience with the criminal justice system. *Social Science Research* 37 (1): 202–19.

Felson, R. B., and J. T. Tedeschi. 1995. A social interactionist approach to violence: Cross-cultural applications. In *Interpersonal violent behaviours*, ed. B. Ruback and N. Weiner, 153–70. New York: Springer.

Fergusson, D. M., L. J. Horwood, and M. T. Lynskey. 1997. Childhood sexual abuse, adolescent sexual behaviors and sexual revictimization. *Child Abuse and Neglect* 21 (8): 789–803.

Finkelhor, D., and L. Baron. 1986. Risk factors for child sexual abuse. *Journal of Interpersonal Violence* 1 (1): 43–71.

Fox, J. A. 1996. *Trends in juvenile violence: A report to the United States Attorney General on current and future rates of juvenile offending.* Report prepared for the Bureau of Justice Statistics. Washington, D.C.: U.S. Department of Justice.

Fuentes, J. 2006. *Practical guide to intelligence-led policing. New Jersey State Police Report.* New York: Manhattan Institute.

Garland, D. 1990. *Punishment and modern society: A study in social theory.* Chicago: University of Chicago Press.

Gau, J. M., and T. C. Pratt. 2008. Broken windows or window dressing? Citizens' (in)ability to tell the difference between disorder and crime. *Criminology and Public Policy* 7 (2): 163–94.

Geis, G. 1986. On the declining crime rate: An exegetic conference report. *Criminal Justice Policy Review* 1:16–36.

Gill, P. 2006. Not just joining the dots but crossing the borders and bridging the voids: Constructing security networks after 11 September 2001. *Policing and Society* 16 (1): 27–49.

Gladwell, M. 2000. *The tipping point: How little things can make a big difference.* Boston: Back Bay Books.

Godfrey and Botelho v. John Doe I et al. No. 01-729, p. 11.

Goetting, A. 1999. *Life stories of women who left abusive men.* New York: Columbia University Press.

Goffman, E. 1959. *The presentation of self in everyday life.* Garden City, N.Y.: Doubleday.

Gottfredson, M., and T. Hirschi. 1990. *A general theory of crime.* Stanford, Calif.: Stanford University Press.

Groff, E. 2007. Simulation for theory testing and experimentation: An example using routine activity theory and street robbery. *Journal of Quantitative Criminology* 23 (2): 75–103.

Harrell, A., and C. Gouvis. 1994. *Predicting neighborhood risk of crime.* Washington, D.C.: National Institute of Justice.

Harries, K. 1999. *Mapping crime: Principles and practice.* Washington, D.C.: National Institute of Justice.

Hart, T. C., and C. Rennison. 2003. *Reporting crime to the police, 1992–2000.* Washington, D.C.: U.S. Department of Justice, Bureau of Justice Statistics.

Hartocollis, A. 2008. Port authority liable in 1993 Trade Center attack. *New York Times*, April 30, 2008.

Hebenton, B., and T. Thomas. 1996. Sexual offenders in the community: Reflections on problems of law, community and risk management in the U.S.A., England and Wales. *International Journal of the Sociology of Law* 24 (4): 427–43.

Interpol. Thai court jails pedophile arrested after Interpol global appeal, at www .interpol.int/Public/THB/vico/Default.asp (accessed July 2008).

Jackson, J. 2006. Introducing fear of crime to risk research. *Risk Analysis* 26 (1): 253–64.

Jacobs, D., and R. E. Helms. 1996. Toward a political model of incarceration: A Time-Series examination of multiple explanations for prison admission rates. *American Journal of Sociology* 102 (2): 323–57.

Janoff-Bulman, R., and I. H. Frieze. 1983. A theoretical perspective for understanding reactions to victimization. *Journal of Social Issues* 39 (2): 1–17.

John, T., and M. Maguire. 2004. *The National Intelligence Model: Early implementation experience in three police force areas.* Working Paper Series 50. Cardiff, UK: Cardiff University, School of Social Sciences.

Johnson, D. 2008. A city's police force now doubts focus on terrorism. *New York Times*, July 24, 2008.

Justice Information Sharing. 2008. Fusion centers and intelligence sharing. U.S. Department of Justice, Office of Justice Programs, at www.it.ojp.gov/default .aspx?area=nationalInitiatives&page=1181 (accessed June 2009).

Kahneman, D., and A. Tversky. 1979. Prospect theory: An analysis of decision under risk. *Econometrica* 47 (2): 263–91.

Kean, T. H., and L. H. Hamilton. 2004. *The 9/11 Commission Report.* Washington, D.C.: National Commission on Terrorist Attacks upon the United States.

Kelling, G., and C. Coles. 1996. *Fixing broken windows.* New York: Touchstone.

Kennedy, D. M., Anthony A. B., A. Piehl, and E. J. Waring. 2001. *Reducing gun violence: The Boston Gun Project's Operation Ceasefire.* Washington, D.C.: U.S. Department of Justice, National Institute of Justice Research Report, NCJ 188741.

Kennedy, L. W., and S. W. Baron. 1993. Routine activities and a subculture of violence: A study of violence on the street. *Journal of Research in Crime and Delinquency* 30 (1): 88–112.

Kennedy, L. W., and D. Forde. 1990. Routine activities and crime: An analysis of victimization in Canada. *Criminology* 28:101–15.

———. 1999. *When push comes to shove: A routine conflict approach to violence.* Albany, N.Y.: State University of New York Press.

Kennedy, L. W., and V. Sacco. 1998. *Crime victims in context.* New York: Oxford University Press.

Kennedy, L. W., and R. A. Silverman. 1985. Perceptions of social diversity and fear of crime. *Environment and Behavior* 17 (3): 275–95.

Kennedy, L. W., and D. Veitch. 1997. Why are the crime rates going down? *Canadian Journal of Criminology* 39 (1): 51–69.

Koverola, C., J. Proulx, P. Battle, and C. Hanna. 1996. Family functioning as predictors of distress in revictimized sexual abuse survivors. *Journal of Interpersonal Violence* 11 (2): 263–80.

Kuchinskas, S. 2008. What limits for warrantless wiretapping? *Internetnews.com,* April 10, at www.internetnews.com/infra/article.php/3739856 (accessed May 6, 2009).

Lascher, E. L., and M. Powers. 2004. September 11 victims, random events, and the ethics of compensation. *American Behavioral Scientist* 48 (3): 281–94.

Levi, R. 2000. The mutuality of risk and community: The adjudication of community notification statutes. *Economy and Society* 29 (4): 578–601.

Lo, C. P. 2004. Testing urban theories using remote sensing. *GIScience and Remote Sensing* 41 (2): 95–115.

Luckenbill, D., and D. Doyle. 1989. Structural position and violence: Developing a cultural explanation. *Criminology* 27 (3): 419–36.

Lum, C., L. W. Kennedy, and A. Sherley. 2006. Are counter-terrorism strategies effective? The results of the Campbell Systematic Review on Counter-terrorism Evaluation Research. *Journal of Experimental Criminology* 2 (4): 489–516.

Maguire, M. 2000. Policing by risks and targets: Some dimensions and implications of intelligence-led crime control. *Policing and Society* 9 (4): 315–36.

Maguire, M., and T. John. 2006. Intelligence led policing, managerialism and community engagement: Competing priorities and the roles of the National Intelligence Model in the UK. *Policing and Society* 16 (1): 67–85.

Maltz, M. D. 1977. Crime statistics: A historical perspective. *Crime and Delinquency* 23 (1): 32–40.

Mason, G. 2007. Hate crime as a moral category: Lessons from the Snowtown case (South Australia). *Australian and New Zealand Journal of Criminology* 40 (3): 249–72.

Mazerolle, L., C. Kadleck, and J. Roehl. 2004. Differential police control at drug-dealing places. *Security Journal* 17 (1): 1–69.

McCahill, M., and C. Norris. 2003. Estimating the extent, sophistication and legality of CCTV in London. In *CCTV*, ed. M. Gill, 51–66. London: Perpetuity Press.

McGarrell, E., S. Chermak, J. Wilson, and M. Corsaro. 2006. Reducing homicide through a "lever-pulling" strategy. *Justice Quarterly* 23 (2): 214–23.

McGarrell, E., J. Freilich, and S. Chermak. 2007. Intelligence-led policing as a framework for responding to terrorism. *Journal of Contemporary Criminal Justice* 23 (2): 142–58.

McGloin, J. M., C. J. Sullivan, A. R. Piquero, and T. C. Pratt. 2007. Local life circumstances and offending specialization/versatility: Comparing opportunity and propensity models. *Journal of Research in Crime and Delinquency* 44 (3): 321–46.

Meier, R., L. W. Kennedy, and V. Sacco. 2001. *The structure and process of crime: Advances in criminological theory.* New Brunswick, N.J.: Transaction Press.

Menard, L. 2001. *The metaphysical club: A story of ideas in America.* New York: Farrar, Straus and Giroux.

Miethe, T., and R. Meier. 1994. *Crime and its social context: Toward an integrated theory of offenders, victims, and situations.* Albany, N.Y.: State University of New York Press.

Mitchell, C. 2008. The killing of murder. *New York Magazine*, January 7.

Moe, A. M. 2007. Silenced voices and structured survival: Battered women's help seeking. *Violence against Women* 13 (7): 676–99.

Muftic, L. R., and J. A. Bouffard. 2007. An evaluation of gender differences in the implementation and impact of a comprehensive approach to domestic violence. *Violence against Women* 13 (1): 46–70.

National Center for Victims of Crime. Repeat victimization, at www.ncvc.org/ncvc/AGP.Net/Components/documentViewer/Download.aspxnz?DocumentID=41161 (accessed July 2008).

National Crime Prevention Council. Neighborhood watch: Tools and resources to help you start or maintain a Neighborhood Watch program, at www.ncpc.org/topics/home-and-neighborhood-safety/neighborhood-watch (accessed June 2009).

New York Civil Liberties Union. 2006. *Who's watching: Video camera surveillance in New York City and the need for public oversight.* New York: Author.

Newburn, T., and T. Jones. 2007. *Policy transfer and criminal justice: Exploring US influence over British crime control policy.* Maidenhead, UK: Open University Press/McGraw Hill.

Norris, C. 2007. The intensification and bifurcation of surveillance in British criminal justice policy. *European Journal on Criminal Policy and Research* 13 (1–2): 139–58.

O'Connell, P. E. 2003. An intellectual history of the Compstat model of police management. *Dissertation Abstracts International, A: The Humanities and Social Sciences* 63 (9): 3366-A–3367-A.

Osborn, D., D. Ellingworth, T. Hope, and A. Trickett. 1996. Are repeatedly victimized households different? *Journal of Quantitative Criminology* 12 (2): 223–45.

Osgood, D. W., and A. L. Anderson. 2004. Unstructured socializing and rates of delinquency. *Criminology* 42 (3): 519–49.

PA News. 2007. High-risk offenders crime rises. Channel 4 News, October 22, at www.channel4.com/news/articles/uk/highrisk+offenders+crime+rises/946547 (accessed July 2008).

Park, R., R. D. McKenzie, and E. Burgess. 1925. *The city: Suggestions for the study of human nature in the urban environment.* Chicago: University of Chicago Press.

Pease, K., and G. Laycock. 1996. *Reducing the heat on hot victims.* Washington, D.C.: Bureau of Justice Statistics, U.S. Department of Justice.

Pence, K. R. 1995. Rate your risk: Evaluate risks in your life, at www.rateyourrisk .org/ (accessed July 2008).

Pizarro, J., S. Chermak, and J. Gruenewald. 2007. Juvenile 'super-predators' in the news: A comparison of adult and juvenile homicides. *Journal of Criminal Justice and Popular Culture* 14 (1): 84–110.

Porter, T. M. 1995. Statistical and social facts from Quetelet to Durkheim. *Sociological Perspectives* 38 (1): 15–26.

Quetelet, A. 1842. *A treatise on man and the development of his facilities.* Trans. R. Knox. Edinburgh: Chambers.

Ratcliffe, J. 2003. *Intelligence-led policing.* Canberra: Australian Institute of Criminology.

———. 2006. A temporal constraint theory to explain opportunity-based spatial offending patterns. *Journal of Research in Crime and Delinquency* 43 (3): 261–91.

Rengert, G. F. 1988. Location of facilities and crime. *Journal of Security Administration* 11 (2): 12–16.

Risen, J., and E. Lichtblau. 2005. Bush lets U.S. spy on callers without courts. *New York Times,* December 16, 2005.

Ritter, A. 2006. Studying illicit drug markets: Disciplinary contributions. *International Journal of Drug Policy* 17 (6): 453–63.

Rosenbaum, D. 1987. The theory and research behind neighborhood watch: Is it a sound fear and crime reduction strategy? *Crime and Delinquency* 33 (1): 103–34.

Rossmo, K. 2000. *Geographic profiling.* Boca Raton, Fla.: CRC Press.

Roundtree, P., and K. C. Land. 2000. The generalizability of multilevel models of burglary victimization: A cross-city comparison. *Social Sciences Research* 29 (2): 284–305.

Sacco, V. 2005. *When crime waves.* Thousand Oaks, Calif.: Sage.

Sacco, V., and L. W. Kennedy. 2002. *The criminal event: Perspectives in space and time.* Belmont, Calif.: Wadsworth.

Sageman, M. 2004. *Understanding terror networks.* Philadelphia: University of Pennsylvania Press.

Sampson, R. J., and W. B. Groves. 1989. Community structure and crime: Testing social disorganization theory. *American Journal of Sociology* 94:774–802.

Sampson, R. J., and J. Laub. 1990. Crime and deviance over the life course: The salience of adult social bonds. *American Sociological Review* 55:609–27.

——. 1993. Turning points in the life course: Why change matters to the study of crime. *Criminology* 31 (3): 301–25.

Sampson, R. J., and S. Raudenbush. 1999. Systematic social observation of public spaces: A new look at disorder in urban neighborhoods. *American Journal of Sociology* 105:603–51.

Shaw, C. R., and H. D. McKay. 1969. *Juvenile delinquency and urban areas*. Chicago: University of Chicago Press.

Sherman, L. W. 1992. *Policing domestic violence: Experiments and dilemmas*. New York: Free Press.

Sherman, L. W., P. R. Gartin, and M. E. Buerger. 1989. Hot spots of predatory crime: Routine activities and the criminology of place. *Criminology* 27:27–55.

Skogan, W. 2008. Broken windows: Why—and how—we should take them seriously. *Criminology and Public Policy* 7 (2): 195–202.

Slovic, P. 2000. *The perception of risk*. London: Earthscan.

Spector, M., and J. Kitsuse. 1973. Toward a sociology of social problems: Social conditions, value-judgments, and social problems. *Social Problems* 20:407–19.

Stanko, E. A. 2000. "Victims R Us: The life history of 'fear of crime' and the politicization of violence." In *Crime, risk and insecurity: Law and order in everyday life and political discourse*, ed. T. Hope and R. Sparks, 13–30. London: Routledge..

Starks, T. 2008. FISA Overhaul Set to Clear Senate. *CQ.com*, June 20, at http://public .cq.com/docs/cqt/news110-000002902405.html (accessed May 6, 2009).

Stucky, Thomas D., and Joseph B. Lang. 2007. A bigger piece of the pie? State corrections spending and the politics of social order. *Journal of Research in Crime and Delinquency* 44 (1): 91–123.

Taylor, H. 1998. Rationing crime: The political economy of criminal statistics since the 1850s. *Economic History Review* 51 (3): 569–90.

Taylor, R. 2000. *Breaking away from broken windows: Baltimore neighborhoods and the nationwide fight against crime, grime, fear, and decline*. New York: Perseus.

Tedeschi, J., and R. Felson. 1994. *Violence, aggression, and coercive actions*. Washington, D.C.: American Psychological Association.

Tewksbury, R., and E. E. Mustaine. 2006. Where to find sex offenders: An examination of residential locations and neighborhood conditions. *Criminal Justice Studies* 19 (1): 61–75.

Tita, G., and E. Griffiths. 2005. Traveling to violence: The case for a mobility-based spatial typology of homicide. *Journal of Research in Crime and Delinquency* 42 (3): 275–308.

Tita, G., J. K. Riley, and P. Greenwood. 1994. *Reducing gun violence: Operation Ceasefire in Los Angeles*. Washington D.C.: National Institute of Justice.

Tversky, A., and D. Kahneman. 1981. The framing of decisions and the psychology of choice. *Science* 211 (4481): 453–58.

United Kingdom Home Office. 2005. Safer schools and hospitals. April 15, at www .crimereduction.homeoffice.gov.uk/toolkits/ssh04.htm (accessed July 2008).

——. 2008. Crime reduction: Providing information and resources for people working to reduce crime in their local area, at www.crimereduction.homeoffice.gov.uk (accessed July 2008).

U.S. Department of Homeland Security. 2006. *National infrastructure protection plan*. Washington, D.C.: Author.

U.S. Department of Justice. 2006. *Fusion center guidelines*. Washington, D.C.: Author, Office of Justice Programs, Department of Homeland Security, at www .it.ojp.gov.

Van Brunschot, E. G., and L. W. Kennedy. 2004. A case study in crime risk: Jane Doe and the Metropolitan Toronto Police Force. *Security Journal* 17 (2): 21–33.

———. 2008. *Risk balance and security*. Thousand Oaks, Calif.: Sage.

Van Dijk, J. J. M., J. N. van Kesteren, and P. Smit. 2007. *Criminal victimisation in international perspective: Key findings from the 2004–2005 ICVS and EU ICS*. Vienna: United Nations Office on Drugs and Culture.

von Hirsch, A. 1984. The ethics of selective incapacitation: Observations on the contemporary debate. *Crime and Delinquency* 30 (2): 175–94.

Walklate, S. 1997. Risk and criminal victimization: A modernist dilemma? *British Journal of Criminology* 37 (1): 35–45.

Walters, W. 2006. Border/control. *European Journal of Social Theory* 9 (2): 187–203.

Warr, M. 1984. Fear of victimization: Why are women and the elderly more afraid? *Social Science Quarterly* 65:681–702.

Weisburd, D. 2008. *Place-based policing*. Vol. 9. Washington D.C.: Police Foundation.

Welsh, B., and D. P. Farrington. 2001. Toward an evidence-based approach to preventing crime. *ANNALS of the American Academy of Political and Social Science* 578 (1): 158–73.

———. 2003. Effects of closed-circuit television on crime. *ANNALS of the American Academy of Political and Social Science* 587 (1): 110–35.

Wilcox, P., K. C. Land, and S. A. Hunt. 2003. *Criminal circumstance: A dynamic, multi-contextual criminal opportunity theory*. New York: Aldine de Gruyter.

Williams, C. A. 2006. Police and the law. In *A companion to nineteenth-century Europe, 1789–1914*, ed. S. Berger, 345–55. Oxford: Blackwell.

Willis, J., S. D. Mastrofski, and D. Weisburd. 2003. *CompStat in practice: An in-depth analysis of three cities*. Washington, D.C.: Police Foundation.

Wilson, R. J., J. E. Picheca, and M. Prinzo. 2007. Evaluating the effectiveness of professionally-facilitated volunteerism in the community-based management of high-risk sexual offenders: Part one: Effects on participants and stakeholders. *Howard Journal* 46 (3): 289–302.

Wolfe, D. A., and P. G. Jaffe. 1999. Emerging strategies in the prevention of domestic violence. *Domestic Violence and Children* 9 (3): 133–44.

Zedner, L. 2003. Too much security? *International Journal of the Sociology of Law* 31 (3): 155–84.

Zimring, F. 1998. *American youth violence*. New York: Oxford University Press.

Index

About the Authors

Leslie W. Kennedy is a University Professor at the Rutgers University School of Criminal Justice and Director of the Rutgers Center on Public Security. He is also a member of the Core Faculty in the Rutgers Division of Global Affairs. His interests relate to different applications of the risk approach to local and global security across different sectors. He is the coauthor (with Erin GibbsVan Brunschot) of *Risk Balance and Security* (2008), which examines how risk is assessed by agencies faced with major hazards including crime, terrorism, environmental disaster, and disease. He is applying this work to examine risk governance, particularly in the context of the globalization of hazards. In addition, at the local level, he is pursuing empirical research on drug markets and shootings in Newark, New Jersey.

Erin Gibbs Van Brunschot is associate professor in the Department of Sociology and Vice Dean in the Faculty of Social Sciences at the University of Calgary. Her primary research interests are in the realms of crime, security, and risk, with specific interests in how individual, organizational, and state orientations to these issues both diverge and converge. In 2008, she authored *Risk Balance and Security* with Leslie W. Kennedy. She is presently working on a project investigating crime and disorder calls-for-service data from police and bylaw service agencies to address security issues as these relate to socio-demographic characteristics of communities.

www.ingramcontent.com/pod-product-compliance
Lightning Source LLC
Chambersburg PA
CBHW071723290326
41932CB00060B/2312